A DAY IN THE LIFE

7th Cavalry: A Memoir

Walt Madigan

DORRANCE
PUBLISHING CO
EST. 1920
PITTSBURGH, PENNSYLVANIA 15238

Dorrance Publishing Co
585 Alpha Drive
Suite 103
Pittsburgh, PA 15238
Visit our website at *www.dorrancebookstore.com*

ISBN: 979-8-88812-165-8
eISBN: 979-8-88812-665-3

Cover design by Kate Melvin
Interior Design by Dorrance Publishing

This is a memoir, a work of creative non-fiction. It reflects the author's present recollections of experiences over time. Some names and characteristics have been changed, some events have been compressed, and some dialogue has been recreated. It is possible and even probable that those involved may have other memories of the same incidents. Artistic license is used to help clarify, reflect, and characterize.

Author's Note:
Throughout my memoir there are passages where I employ language to describe enemy Vietnamese soldiers as "gooks," "dinks," and "slopes." There is good reason for this: quite simply, this is the way American combat soldiers referred to the enemy whether out in the bush or back at base camp between Search and Destroy missions. It was a by-product of the resentment soldiers felt since most GIs in Vietnam were forced to fight a war in which they wanted no part. Hence, most American soldiers in Charlie Company were not there by choice.

Times have changed; however, and it's been close to fifty years since the war in Vietnam ended. Presently, I harbor no resentment toward the people of Vietnam; nor do I use defamatory language in describing the people of that nation. My mantra nowadays is "Live and Let Live." Any nation such as Vietnam that exists in peace and does not go to war with its neighbors has my utmost respect.

To Nellie, who now sleeps with the angels. Thank you, Mom, for your unconditional love and fierce determination to create free-thinking independent children—all eight of us. And most of all, thank you for teaching me what really matters in life.

Chapter One

Kishine Barracks

On a bright sunny morning in early May 1967, a pretty Air Force nurse approached as I lay in my patient bed at Tachikawa Air Force Base in Japan.

"Private First Class Madigan?"

"That's me, Ma'am," I replied.

"I'm Lt. Russell, your physical therapist for the next three weeks."

This news brought a smile to my lips. I had been recovering from several surgeries that had taken place during the prior month. I had been wounded in my left hip/buttock area in early April from enemy shrapnel after my company walked into a North Vietnamese Army (NVA) ambush in a province outside the city of Song Mao in South Vietnam. The larger chunks of shrapnel had been removed the next day at an Army field hospital in Nha Trang. I was shipped off to the Philippines for minor surgeries to remove several small pieces lodged in my lower extremities, and afterward, I was sent to my current location.

The therapist returned my smile. "Tomorrow you will be transferred to the Army 106th General Hospital at Kishine Barracks in Yokohama. We have a support team there with military physical therapists. You've been assigned to our section along with other recovering soldiers."

I felt my heart sink and my smile fade. I knew the Army hospital in Yokohama would never measure up to the comforts I had experienced the past few weeks, first at Clark Air Force Base in the Philippines, and in Tachikawa. I also knew that in all likelihood, the sooner I healed, the sooner I would be transferred back to my infantry unit in Vietnam. The war in Southeast Asia had only worsened. Within my two-month period in Nam, I had recovered from a smaller wound and been sent back. This second wound was worse and taking longer to heal. If they sent me to battle again, I might not be as lucky the third time I engaged in a firefight with the enemy.

I sat up and Lt. Russell examined my left side from the hip down. She had me execute a few maneuvers while she scribbled on her notepad. Sure enough, early the next morning I was placed on a gurney and loaded onto an Army CH-47 Chinook transport helicopter along with a few badly burned Marines. The chopper rose and I said a silent goodbye in gratitude for the creature comforts I left behind.

We flew to the nearby 106th Army Hospital at Kishine Barracks, an outpost overlooking the city of Yokohama. The Chinook transport helicopter made a slow swoop and settled as smooth as an elevator onto a landing pad painted with a red cross in the center. Surrounding the pad were gray, three-story buildings. I was transferred to a bay with other soldiers with wounds similar to mine—men who would eventually heal and be reassigned to other duty.

Every morning after breakfast, Army nurses would transport me and several other men in wheelchairs to the Physical Therapy building across the quad from the hospital. Lieutenant Russell was there to put me through my paces: stretching and riding a stationary bicycle. She didn't hold back on the strenuous nature of the therapy, and every so often I would break a stitch or two by showing a little too much enthusiasm while trying to impress her. I was rapidly developing a crush on this woman and always looked forward to my morning routines. She was so kind and patient, as well as a beautiful, intelligent, and dedicated officer.

When therapy ended, we spent time engaged in long conversations and she allowed me to call her by her first name, Catherine, when other personnel or officers were not present. Eventually, I found out she was married. Her husband was an infantry officer assigned to the First Infantry Division, also known as the Big Red One, in Vietnam.

Sometimes she asked me what combat was like. Looking into her eyes, I could see the worry, so I toned down my rhetoric. "Oh hell, Catherine, most of the time you are bored senseless out there humping a ruck in the bush and dealing with the heat and bugs. You hardly ever see the enemy, and if things heat up, well…you get on the horn and call in artillery; or, better yet, call in an air strike. Nothing like two F-4 Phantom jet fighter-bombers soaring overhead to brighten your day," I said with conviction. "And let me tell you, L-T, when those fast movers show up, flying maybe thirty or forty meters above the jungle canopy, and bring the damn damn down on Chas, you know which side you'd rather be on."

"Chas?" she asked.

"That's short for Charlie. That's what we called the gooks. If you mention the enemy, Viet Cong, and shorten it to VC, and use the military phonetic alphabet as Victor Charlie, that's how you come up with Charlie."

Her eyes grew misty as she smiled and squeezed my hand. I'm not sure if I made her feel better. On more than one occasion, I could see her eyes moisten with tears. I decided not to talk about the war after that.

. . .

Later in the day, most of us grunts received our second ration of pain pills. I would take a long nap after the exhaustive physical therapy. One Sunday afternoon, I was awakened by a USO service volunteer who entered our bay and announced that we had a special visitor. In through the double doors walked the entertainer, Andy Williams, followed by composer, Henry Mancini, who wheeled in an upright piano on flat furniture dollies. He was followed by Williams' beautiful wife, Claudine Longet, a French recording star and actress. Every man in the bay gasped when they saw her. Dressed in a white mini-dress with her smooth, long hair cascading over her shoulders, she looked like a petite angel descended from heaven. Andy Williams was a huge star in Japan at that time. His Sunday night show was the only TV program to be simultaneously broadcast in English as well as Japanese. Luckily for us, he was on a promotional tour in Japan and had decided to come over and entertain the injured soldiers at the 106th.

Williams sang most of his current hits a cappella including "Moon River" and "Let it Be Me." Occasionally, Mancini would accompany him on the piano, and Longet joined him for a duet. Afterward, Williams and Mancini walked up to each bed in the ward and shook hands with every wounded soldier and offered a few words of encouragement. Longet followed carrying a large bouquet of roses and placed a single flower at the foot of every bed. Then she gazed directly into each soldier's eyes and mouthed the words "Thank you." I could feel my heart melt when she glanced at me with her dark liquid eyes. She smiled demurely and laid a single rose on my sheet.

Chapter Two

CQ

After a month of being in and out of various hospitals with a regimen of intense physical therapy, I started to heal at an accelerated pace. The doctors at the 106th decided to replace my wire stitches, which were downright torturous, with threaded cotton sutures—the difference like moving from a dungeon to a day spa. Soon I was able to get about with a slight limp, and shed the wheelchair and cane. I still looked forward to my daily ration of pain pills, especially after a change of dressings on my upper leg.

I watched with fascination as my assigned nurse gingerly removed the layers of bandages, while another nurse squirted a saline solution on the wound to help unstick the dressings. As she released each thin cotton wrap, I was amazed at the different colors of fluid that came out of my body: green and yellow slime mixed with blood and clear serous discharge surrounding the ugly stitched-up hole.

"Are those fluids normal?" I asked.

"Yes, soldier," she said cheerfully, as if snotty-looking pus was a rainbow in disguise. "You're healing up fine and will be as good as new in no time. Most of that scar will eventually disappear."

Soon I became friends with the lieutenant assigned to night CQ (Charge of Quarters) for my ward. Lieutenant Mark Coleman was a first-year intern from Maryland. He had attended an Ivy League university followed by the University of Maryland Medical School. He joined ROTC in his junior year of college, sensing he would be drafted after medical school, and hoped he would be assigned to a hospital outside the war zone. I was a bit of a night owl, and enjoyed Lt. Coleman's company in the late evenings.

After dinner I would often join him in his office, which was located outside my bay. His shift ran from 6:00 p.m. to 6:00 a.m. The L-T taught me how to play chess. He enjoyed hearing the stories I told of growing up in a large blue-collar, working-class, Irish Catholic family. His background could not have been more different than my own; however, he never put on airs. I was into the surfing scene as the whole Southern California surfing phenomena took shape in the early sixties. He would goad me into telling stories of what it was like, and he especially wanted to hear about the surfer babes.

"Listen, L-T," I said, "those girls weren't exactly like the ones you saw in *Beach Blanket Bingo*."

I told Lt. Coleman about one girl who stood out from the rest, a real beauty named Christine. She was a senior at nearby Santa Monica High School, and when she showed up at our surfing spot, most of the guys got weak in the knees. She had dirty blonde hair, an impressive tan and a sculpted body. Rather than stare outright, we would pretend to wax our surfboards or read tide charts as she stripped down to a skimpy black bikini to sunbathe on her towel.

When the surf got blown out, usually around noon, my buddies and I went on a scavenger hunt underneath the creaky wooden boards of the Santa Monica Pier to find the coldest, ugliest corpse of a fish. This was something we did from time to time. Then we would wait for the surfer girls to lay face down on their towels and reach back to undo their bikini tops in order to eliminate tan lines. That was the moment we would sneak up and lay that disgusting item along their warm backsides. Invariably, they would scream and jump off their towels forgetting to tie their tops. That was always fun.

As the sun set, we would build a huge bonfire on the beach, break out our cheap wine, and talk about everything and anything under the stars. Waves rolled up in a hypnotic rhythm and wind rustled through the palm trees. In the distance you could hear the whoosh of cars on Highway One. Those were times we felt we had come into the world at the right time and enjoyed teenaged life the best way we knew how.

"Anyway," I said to the L-T, "the president of our surf club, Mike Jacobs, had a crush on Christine and one night, he kept pestering her for a little kiss. Mike was a damn good surfer, but the poor guy had terrible acne on his face and most of his body, especially his back. He usually wore an old tattered tuxedo jacket and a black top hat while surfing, probably to distract from his skin problem. His stunts were amazing and he had his photo in Surfer Magazine a few times, which made him a local celebrity.

"So after growing tired of hearing Mike pester her, Christine stood up and walked over to him. You could tell she was still rankled about the dead fish incident earlier that day. 'Okay,' she said. 'Just a little kiss…but only if I can find a smooth spot.' Ouch! I guess he had it coming."

· · ·

On most evenings, I assisted Lt. Coleman as he made his rounds on the entire third floor of our building. I helped in dispensing meds, checking pulses, taking temperatures, and hooking up IVs, among other chores. I talked to the injured soldiers and in turn, listened to their stories. I would inject a little humor (pun intended) to try and cheer them up.

When the Catholic chaplin assigned to the 106th, Father William O' Donoghue, would join us, he handed out rosaries and religious pamphlets. After a while, we called him Father Bill. I had spirited conversations with him in the small Catholic chapel after saying a rosary every morning before breakfast. A Minnesotan, Father Bill had attended the St. Paul Seminary School of Divinity. He was first generation Irish, and his parents were immigrants from County Clare in Ireland.

"Madigan, huh?" he said one night. "That's as common a name in County Clare as Smith is in America."

He ingrained in me a sense of hope, and told me my faith in God would get me through the tough times. He told me to never even think of giving up. "Life is a test," he said. " 'Blessed is the man who remains steadfast under trial, for when he has stood the test, he will receive the crown of life, which God has promised to those who love him' (James 1:12). Remember that, son."

I was fortunate to have come from a large, loving, concerned family and received copious amounts of mail each week. Many of these wounded warriors had little or no family or girlfriends to wish them well or send packages filled with cookies or treats. I could tell from the expression on the faces of these unfortunate comrades that things were not going to get better soon; they would lay in bed, almost comatose, and stare blankly at the overhead ceiling fans. It didn't take me long to realize that the wounds I suffered in combat were a mere toothache in comparison. Many of these soldiers were missing limbs and others had oversized colostomy bags attached to their guts. I thought about the soldiers wounded next to me during that fateful enemy ambush on April 4th. Some clutched their stomachs to keep their intestines from spilling onto the jungle floor. A few cried out for their mothers before dying amidst the chaos.

One night, Lt. Coleman pulled me aside. He said I had been doing a good job as his aide, but cautioned me not to talk about the war with any of his patients. "Besides, Private Madigan," he said as he put his arm around my shoulder, "you seem to have a wealth of stories about growing up in Southern California. They're hilarious. That's what these soldiers need to hear. Most of these men are going home one day, and they need to hear stories that will give them hope, and I must say you're damn good at providing exactly that."

"Gee, thanks, L-T," I said. I felt a small flush of embarrassment, but was thankful for the compliment.

Chapter Three

Roachman

A few nights later, the L-T and I were about finished with our rounds when I heard a deep baritone voice call out, "Hey, Madigan, that you, man?"

I looked around and saw a large Black man sitting up in the last bed by the bay doors. The bulk of his head was wrapped in a massive dressing, and his right arm was in a cast from shoulder to wrist and suspended with wires attached to the ceiling. As I approached his bed, I recognized him as a soldier from my platoon in Charlie Company, Sgt. Roach, one of our machine gunners.

"Jesus, Mary, and Joseph," I exclaimed. "Roachman! I can't believe it's you. Holy shit. The last time I saw you, Lt. Anderson and I had gotten hit by that Chicom and were pinned down by AK fire. You came charging by totin' that M60 with bandoleers of ammo flying around your neck. I wish you could have seen yourself—eyeballs as big as flying saucers, and this crazed look on your face. Your ammo bearers could hardly keep up with you."

At our first meeting, I had felt intimidated by Sgt. Leland Roach. He stood six feet four inches and was built like a Black Hercules. He rarely wore a shirt and would strut about our base camp with a black do-rag on his head and a dirty green Army-issue towel around his neck. He would carry his M60 machine gun in one hand as if it were a plastic toy, and in his other, he would perch a large 8-track player on his shoulder as it pumped out tunes from the Temptations, Stevie Wonder, and Marvin Gaye. He hailed from somewhere in the Deep South. Once he became your friend, you were allowed to call him Roachman, which seemed appropriate since he loved to smoke "Black Mo" when we returned to base camp for a little R and R after a Search and Destroy mission.

"Yeah, Madigan," he said in a subdued tone. "We got our asses kicked that day, but not before I took out at least six or seven of them fuckin' dinks. Then ol' Charlie sent one of them B40 rocket-propelled grenades right at my position. Mothafucka exploded right in front of me and took out a good piece of my shoulder and elbow, and damn near sheared off my right ear. I also took some frags in my gut."

Using his good left hand, he pulled aside his pajama top so I could see the tubes attached to a colostomy bag. Whatever emotion I might have shown was broken by the entrance of the L-T and Father Bill.

"Sgt. Roach, I would like to introduce you to Lt. Coleman, the night CQ for your bay, and Father William O' Donoghue. You can call him Father Bill if you want. He's great guy. If you believe in a higher power, Roachman, and I happen to know that you do, then talk to Father Bill."

Lt. Coleman squeezed Sgt. Roach's left hand and exchanged a few pleasantries. Then he got down to the business of checking out the sergeant's chart. I assisted the L-T as he changed out Roach's colostomy bag. I had not seen this procedure, which was fascinating to watch, and once again, I felt blessed for the minor wounds I suffered.

"Hey, Madigan," Sgt. Roach said, "you ever tell the L-T or Father Bill about that show you put on for us at the beach in Phan Thiêt? Shee-it, Lieutenant. We came back from a grueling Search and Destroy, and most of the boonie rats in Charlie Company plopped down and went to sleep in their hooch, or maybe they cleaned up and got some hot chow. But not Ol' Surfer Joe here. He just peeled off his filthy fatigues, put his trunks on and goes out catching waves on the beach like he's back in Malibu or somethin'. Shee-it. He could care less that there was a war goin' on."

He let out one of his huge bellowing laughs, "Heh! Heh! Heh!

"And then that night at mail call," he continued. "Man, you was some kind of hero."

"Aw, fuck it, Roachman. Don't mean nothin.'"

"Maybe not to you, Surfer Joe," he said, "but it sure meant somethin' to those guys in Second Platoon. You did real good that night, Madigan."

"Thanks, Sergeant."

Lt. Coleman nudged me that it was time to move on.

"Listen, Roachman, rest up and get well. Looks like you'll be going home soon and won't be totin' that M60 for a long time."

"What about you, Madigan?"

"Me? Shit, all I got was a scratch compared to you and most of those guys in Charlie Company. I'll probably get reassigned back to Second Platoon in a few weeks. I'll be sure to tell all those boonie rats that I ran into you, and that you're doin' fine."

I was sure my eyes looked glassy. "And Roachman," I added, "I still have that rosary my mother gave me before I left for the Nam. I try and make it down to the chapel every morning before chow, and I'll be sure to include you in my prayers."

Now he had tears streaming down his face. I was about to turn and leave when Sgt. Roach grabbed my arm.

"God bless you, Madigan," he cried. "God bless you, man."

Chapter Four

On the Mend

For weeks, I had been dreading this day. The Chief Medical Officer at 106th General Hospital decided I was well enough to be transferred. I moved across the quad from my hospital ward to Building C, a housing barracks within the Kishine complex where I would await further reassignment.

I took my place on the third floor where a somber and tense mood prevailed. Most of these soldiers were grunts like me and we were not looking forward to returning to our respective units in Vietnam. Some men sat on their bunks reading pulp novels. Others had a smoke or played solitaire; some wrote letters home. One thing we all had in common was that thousand-yard stare as we languished for days waiting to hear our next assignment. Twenty-seven hundred miles to the southwest, the war in Vietnam was still raging, and there was no end in sight.

I became friends with another foot soldier who shared the bunk above mine. Specialist 4th Class Kevin Green was a medic with the 101st Airborne Division, the Screaming Eagles. Generally, 101st Airborne guys and First Air Cav soldiers did not get along, and small altercations could escalate into brawls at the NCO clubs on any given night.

One night I sat with a few Air Cav friends at the NCO club, which was attached to Kishine Barracks. We were having a good time drinking beer and flirting with the Japanese girls while listening to a local Japanese rock band, and the change of pace took my mind off the minor surgery I'd had that morning. In seconds, a squabble exploded in size. I was in a wheelchair and had to duck as bottles of beer were flung back and forth. One Screaming Eagle sergeant was so infuriated, he grabbed our table and tipped it over, sending beer bottles, lit cigarettes, and ashtrays flying everywhere. Seeing me helpless, Specialist Green rushed to my aid, grabbed the handles of my wheelchair, and wheeled me to safety in a corner of the bar.

"That pissed off sergeant was getting ready to tip you next," he laughed. "You're lucky a Screaming Eagle rescued your sorry Air Cav ass," Green said.

"Yeah. Thanks, man."

After the fray, Green headed up to the bar, grabbed two fresh beers, and we sat and talked for hours. Kevin was from upstate New York, and like Lt. Coleman, loved hearing stories about surf culture in Southern California. His wounds were similar to mine and we were both on the mend.

. . .

Every morning after breakfast a transportation sergeant named Brooks would enter our barracks. He always seemed to have a joke or two for the men before roll call. Then he would call out specific names and inform those men that they were being transferred out that afternoon or early evening. They would get their official packets by noon, and most of them were sent back to Vietnam.

Eventually, I was able to scrounge a decent pair of fatigues and new combat boots from the local supply sergeant at Kishine. There was no way in hell I was returning to my unit in Army-issue pajamas; I was tired of shuffling around the barracks looking like a gook in those lame-ass pj's, and I knew it wouldn't be long before I heard Brooks call my name.

I found it puzzling that Brooks, a tall Black staff sergeant lifer in his mid-thirties, was so casual about his appearance. He wore his hair in a semi-fro with a hair pick sticking out the side and his baseball cap tilted askew. Even though his fatigues were usually pressed, they were always a mismatched shade of Army green, and shined boots were beyond his notice.

I remembered something my platoon sergeant in the Nam once told me while we were out on a night ambush. "You know, Madigan, you might think it's the majors or colonels, or even the generals who wield all the power in this man's Army. But don't be fooled, man. It's the supply and transportation sergeants who really get things done, and ultimately, they wield the real power. Believe me; you never want to piss these guys off."

One morning, Sgt. Brooks called my name after roll call.

"Here," I answered. I felt a lump in my throat. This was it.

Brooks looked up from his clipboard and stared at me for several seconds. He looked back at his clipboard, and said. "Whatcha doin' wearin' those fatigues, soldier?"

"Look, Sarge," I said. "I'll be damned if I'm returning to my unit in the Nam wearing those ugly-ass Army-issue pajamas and slippers, looking like some sorry-ass dink."

Again, he looked over the top of his clipboard and this time, sized me up with a glare. "Come over here, Private."

I walked up and he handed me his clipboard.

"Do you see your name on that list, Private Madigan?" I read down the list until I spotted my name followed by my serial number and the last unit I served with in Vietnam: Company C, 2nd Bn, 7th Inf, 1st Cav Div (Airmobile).

"I see my name, Sergeant."

"Okay, that's good," Brooks said. "Now tell me what it says after that." A sly smile crossed his face as he scanned the other men in the barracks.

And as I reviewed the contents on his clipboard, in that moment, my brain shone a thread of light on what Sgt. Brooks was up to. My body trembled with a slight twinge of hope. After my named division where I served in Vietnam, the orders read: Evac: Trans from Tach Air Force Base, Japan: 2100 hrs on C-141 Starlifter Med Transport, Dest: Travis Air Force Base, Fairfield, CA. Re: further eval of frag wounds: left hip/buttock; left leg/knee; lower extremities. The orders were signed by the Chief Medical Officer of the 106th Hospital, and near the bottom of those orders, I saw Lt. Coleman's signature.

I stood there, stunned. "I don't understand, Sergeant. What does this mean?"

"WHAT'S THAT MEAN?" He shouted so every man in the barracks could hear him. "IT MEANS YOU IS GOIN' BACK TO THE WORLD! That's what that mean, soldier. You goin' back to The World tonight when they load you up on that medical C-141 Starlifter at 2100 hours."

I felt something like an adrenaline rush and thought I was going to faint from the ineffable joy flowing through my veins. I stared at those orders, dumbfounded, thinking there must be a mistake.

Sgt. Brooks smirked as he gauged my reaction and decided to play up the moment.

"Listen here, Private First Class Madigan, if I was you, I would ditch those fatigues and combat boots before the CMO walks in here and sees you ready to go back to the Nam, 'cuz maybe he change his mind. It says here they will be wheeling you out on a gurney and loading you up on one of those Army Medical Shithooks to transfer yo' ass over to Tachikawa so they can load you up on one of those monster C-141 Starlifter medical ships. So you best get yo' self back into a pair of those UGLY-ASS blue pajamas!"

Brooks didn't need to say another word. I rushed to a hamper by the bay doors and tried to get out of my fatigue shirt. I was so excited, my fingers fumbled around with the buttons as if they were new to me. "Fuck this!" I ripped open the shirt, and heard buttons clatter across the shiny tile floor. I knocked off my combat boots as fast as humanly possible and sat on the floor to peel off my fatigue pants. I threw everything into an empty hamper. Standing there naked, except for a small dressing and bandages attached to my left hip, I walked over to another hamper filled with discarded pajamas. A small circle of blood began to seep through the dressings over my wounds, probably from popping a stitch or two in my excitement. I realized how quiet the room had become, and turned to see Sgt. Brooks and every man in the barracks staring at me in disbelief.

"Let me ask you sumptin," Brooks said. "What happened to you, soldier?"

"I got hit by a Chicom, Sergeant," I said while rummaging through the hamper to find a pair of pj's in my size.

"A Chicom?" inquired Brooks.

"A Chinese manufactured hand grenade."

"How long was you in combat?"

"I don't know, uh, maybe two months."

"Shee-it." Brooks chuckled and the morning sun glinted off his gold-capped teeth. "You can't fool me, mista. I know what happened to you. You done saw that grenade land and then you stuck your big ol' cherry ass up in the air to catch ol' Charlie's flak."

Some of the men in the barracks laughed, and Green, my bunkmate, yelled out, "That's what he did, Sergeant. He stuck his big old

Irish ass in the air and caught old Charlie's flak." The room exploded into laughter.

Sgt. Brooks was getting on my last nerve, but I remembered what Sgt. Porter said about transportation sergeants and the influence they carried over men's lives. In desperation, I found a pair of pajamas that looked close to my size and threw them on. They were pretty funky from body fluid stains, but at that point I didn't care if the last guy wearing them had leprosy.

"Well, what do you think, Sarge?" I posed as if modeling a new outfit in front of a girlfriend. Brooks gave me the once-over as he pulled out his hair pick and fluffed up his fro.

"What about slippers?" he asked.

"Under my bed, Sarge."

He smiled and chuckled to himself. "Well, I guess you good to go, soldier." He told me to be back at my bed by 1900 hours with any small possessions I could carry. "You definitely don't want to miss that Shithook, Private Madigan." He put on his cap and exited the barracks.

Chapter Five

Tea Garden

I walked back to my bed, grabbed my shave bag, and took out my rosary before heading to the Catholic chapel attached to the main hospital. Upon entering the 106th, first I decided to tell Sgt. Roach the good news. Ascending the steps, I felt like I was floating on air. His bed was empty, stripped of its sheets. I looked around, expecting to see him in a wheelchair, something. The ward nurse informed me that Sergeant Leland Roach had been transferred the night before to Walter Reed Army Medical Hospital in Washington, D.C., and that Lt. Coleman had taken a three-day leave to Kyoto, the ancient Imperial capital of Japan.

Since the Roachman was no longer around, I did the next best thing and made my way to the chapel. I was the only soul in the dimly lit room. I knelt in a front pew and said the rosary as I tried to do on most mornings if I was not assigned to light duty. I prayed for all my fellow boonie rats in Charlie Company, both living and dead. I prayed for the Roachman and all the other poor souls in the hospital here and elsewhere. I prayed for my family, and last of all, prayed that I would have a safe journey home.

I sat for a while and gazed at the altar, at Christ hanging from the cross, the palms of his hands nailed to the wooden crossbeams with huge spikes, his eyes turned upward in agony and a nest of thorns fastened to his head. Blood trickled down the sides of his face. *Thank you, God. Thank you, God,* I repeated in my mind. *Thank you, God, for my life.* As I prayed, I felt an unknown sensation fill me. My heart felt as though it could burst from my chest; it was like I had been reborn. I never thought it was possible to feel a euphoria that elevated my whole being, as if it had reached inside me, physically, emotionally, and into my soul. Deep down, I knew that if I was to be sent back to my unit in Vietnam, I would most certainly die, or at the very least, be horribly wounded.

. . .

Outside the chapel was a beautiful park arranged like a Japanese tea garden. I went there often to escape the funereal atmosphere of Building C. The park was laced with stone walkways leading to areas of sunken gardens, small waterfalls, and clusters of Japanese wisteria and dwarf pines. Cherry Blossom trees were in full bloom with bright pink flowers that seemed to glow with an inner light. I found a bench next to an arched bridge that spanned a pond filled with brightly colored koi fish.

The park was meticulously maintained by two Japanese groundsmen. They would smile at me and perform a small bow as was their custom. I would smile back at them, put my hands together as though I were praying, and bow in their direction.

The 106th Hospital and Kishine Barracks were located high atop a hill and sitting on that particular bench, I was able to look down upon the city of Yokohama and the Bay of Tokyo. Across the bay I could see the port city of Kisarazu on the Boso Peninsula, and beyond the peninsula, the deep blue Pacific Ocean, and further still, beyond the shimmering horizon…The World.

I relaxed, closed my eyes, and let all thoughts drift from my mind as the mid-morning sun bathed my body. A light breeze floated in from the northwest, and I could smell the sweet floral scent of the cherry blossoms. Behind me, I could hear the soft burble from the waterfall empty into the pond and the occasional splash from a koi fish as it leaped for flying insects. I never felt so alive in my life.

I would be going back to the US mainland tonight and not return to the ugly face of war. The world seemed full of possibilities. When I opened my eyes, I looked at the cerulean blue sky decorated with small clouds puffs drifting over Tokyo Bay, each cloud white as snow and freshly minted by God Himself.

Just one more moment in time, Dear God,...one more moment, Lord Jesus,...to be able to walk through the door of that small house on Marvin Avenue, to look into my mother's beautiful blue eyes, to feel her embrace as she kisses my cheek and welcomes me home, to sit once again at the dining room table while she smokes a Marlboro, drinks Lucky Lager, and throws her head back with that wonderful throaty laugh. And to be reunited with my brothers and sisters one more time, to look into their eyes, to see their faces and hear their laughter as they tell their stories. Just one more moment...

. . .

"Hey, Madigan, whatcha' doin', man?"

Specialist Green headed my way with a tan packet in his hand. "Nothing much. Watching clouds float over Tokyo Bay."

Green held the packet in front of my face. "I got my reassignment orders," he said. "Guess where I'm heading? Guam. Can you believe that? Like, where in the fuck is Guam?"

"I think it's a small island in the Pacific, yeah, somewhere between here and Hawaii. I do know, Green, that Guam is where those Arc Light missions originate. Those B-52 bombers flying up in the stratosphere, 30,000 feet above the enemy and then unloading thirty tons of bombs. God, Green, it's like: SURPRISE, MOTHERFUCKER! Ol' Charlie Viet Cong never knew what hit him, his shit scattered to the wind: north, south, east, west. We could feel the earth shake and hear the rumble of those strikes a good ten miles away."

"What the hell am I going to do in Guam?" Green asked, mainly to himself. "Inoculate the natives? Anyway, it's better than going back to that shithole, Vietnam."

"You got that right, my friend."

"I gotta tell you, Madigan, that was some hell of a performance you put on this morning in the barracks, stripping off those fatigues like they were on fire."

"I had no idea I was going back to the states. I still won't believe it until I'm in the belly of that C-141 Starlifter."

"Oh, you can believe it. Your transfer packet is on your bunk. I took a little peek. Hope you don't mind. That Starlifter Medical Ship is scheduled to take off at 2100 hours." Green stood and looked at his watch. "Hey, I'm going to get some chow at the mess hall. Want to join me?"

"No thanks, Green. I'm going to sit here awhile. I'll catch up with you later back at the barracks.

"Suit yourself, man," he said. He reached out with his right hand and made a fist to exchange a dap, a soul handshake comprised of various slaps and snaps of the hands that only grunts seemed to know.

Chapter Six

Ambush

I sat back on my bench, relaxed, and thought about my fellow boonie rats in Charlie Company. One guy in particular came to mind, our medic in Second Platoon, Specialist 4th Class Angelo "Angel" Martinez, or as Sgt. Porter dubbed him, the "Mad Mexican."

I thought about the first time I got hit in combat. It was no biggie, not even close to the wounds I would receive six weeks later that would get me sent back to The World. In fact, I never mentioned getting wounded that first time in my letters home. I'm sure my mother and family were stressed out enough and did not to need to hear about that slight incident. Even so, it was enough to get me temporarily sidelined.

I was out on my second Search and Destroy mission, and we were humping in mountainous terrain about six klicks northwest of our home base in Phan Thiêt. Second Platoon was flanking the side of a ridge—we did our best to stay off marked trails for obvious reasons—when our point man, Bill Brueland, stopped in his tracks and raised his right hand, palm forward, fingers pointing to the sky. He slowly curled his fingers down until his hand formed a fist, and tweaked his wrist back and forth five times. Every member of Charlie Company froze in place; Brueland's hand signal meant one thing: enemy ahead, fifty meters.

Sgt. Porter blew past me like silent wind, followed by our machine gunner, Sgt. Roach and his two ammo bearers, and then Lt. Anderson and his radio operator. Porter dropped his ruck to the jungle floor, pulled out a pair of field binoculars, and surveyed the scene in front of him. In seconds, Sgt. Roach had his M60 machine gun set up on a tripod as his ammo bearers laid out several bandoleers of shiny, copper 7.62 millimeter bullets, each belt holding a hundred rounds and ready to be fed into his weapon.

Lt. Anderson grabbed the handset of the PRC-25 radio and whispered information at a frenzied pace to our Commanding Officer, Captain Hudson, who was still to our rear. Sgt. Porter turned and looked at me, his face streaked with camouflage paint that blended in with the surrounding foliage. He raised his right hand and flashed five fingers, closed his hand, and flashed three more fingers, reclosed his hand into a fist and tweaked it left to right three times. Finally, he reached up and touched his nose: pass it on.

I turned and relayed Sgt. Porter's message to the men behind me: enemy approaching, squad of eight VC, out thirty meters, lock and load.

My heart pounded in my ears as I reached down with exacting deliberation and unfastened all four ammo pouches attached to my web gear. In slow motion, I dropped to one knee and laid out twelve magazines in an elliptical pattern, which roughly coordinated with my field of fire. I wanted to be ready when the show started. It was rare for Charlie Company to get the drop on the VC.

I saw Brueland raise his M16 and nestle the rifle stock in the hollow of his shoulder. To him, soldiering was a sober occupation and he pretty much kept to himself. After being in-country two weeks and assigned to the First Cav, his father sent him a special 4X scope, which he somehow managed to attach to his M16 rifle. I knew Brueland from Infantry Jungle Training at Tigerland in Louisiana. He came from Waco, Texas, another hunter in a long line of outdoorsmen. He was born with a hunter's instinct. Sgt. Porter made a good call putting him on point that day.

Brueland made one or two adjustments to his scope while Sgt. Porter and Lt. Anderson brought their rifles up into firing position. At the ready, Brueland switched his M16 to full automatic and opened fire.

All hell broke loose! A fusillade of ear-deafening gunfire filled the air. I hit the jungle floor and felt a stabbing pain in my upper left thigh. I figured I hit a tree stump or other sharp protuberance, but stayed down as rifle fire clattered in all directions. Rounds whizzed over my head and branches snapped from the large jackfruit tree to my rear. Enemy AK-47s fired in our direction made a distinct popping sound, followed by the roar of our M16s—most of them on full automatic—and Sgt. Roach's M60 machine gun as it returned punishing fire.

I heard the distinct chatter of Vietnamese to my right and watched as three dinks clamored up the ridge opposite me. Two carried AK-47s and one had an RPG (rocket propelled grenade) strapped across his back. I slid a fresh magazine into my 16, switched to full automatic, and opened fire through the dense foliage. I'm not sure I hit anyone, but it felt good to have them on the run.

"CEASE FIRE!"

I recognized Sgt. Porter's voice and saw him rise while dusting himself off. Though the surrounding area was devoid of sound, Second Platoon waited, frozen on the jungle floor. The smell of burning cordite permeated the air. When the smoke cleared, and it was safe to move about, Porter, Brueland, Lt. Anderson and Capt. Hudson meandered forward to assess the damage. We claimed a small victory of four dead enemy soldiers. Porter discovered two blood trails. He gathered two squads from Second Platoon and took off in hot pursuit.

Fortunately, we suffered no casualties, or so I thought. I stood and brushed the debris off my fatigues, grateful we had survived, even as the rest of the platoon charged ahead.

Caswell looked me over. "Hey, Madigan. What the fuck happened to you?" He gestured at my left thigh. Looking down, I saw my fatigues on that side were drenched in blood. Caswell shouted, "MEDIC!" and along came Specialist 4th Class Angelo "Angel" Martinez.

· · ·

When I was first assigned to the Cav, I had to go through an intense week-long jungle training course in An Khe, the home base of the First Cavalry Division (Airmobile) in Vietnam. Randy Caswell and Randy Kent were two buddies who went through Tigerland with me at Ft. Polk. We had all come from Southern California and ended up in the same squad. Afterwards, we were assigned to Charlie Company, loaded up on a large CH-47 Chinook transport helicopter and flown to the coastal town of Phan Thiêt, where the 2nd Division of the 7th Cavalry was in charge of guarding an airstrip named LZ Betty. This landing zone ran parallel to the South China Sea and was built by the French in the late 1950s. The French began colonization of Vietnam as early as the 1880s; it lasted six decades. They met with disaster in 1954 when the French-held garrison at Dien Bien Phu fell after a four-month siege by Vietnamese nationalist Ho Chi Minh. The French pulled out of Vietnam shortly thereafter.

The 7th Cavalry was nicknamed "Garryowen" for an Irish jig that can be traced back to the 1860s, and adopted by various militaries as its march tune. The 7th Cavalry dates to a time before George Armstrong Custer's regiment that was wiped out in the Battle of the Little Big Horn in June of 1876. Leap forward, and in Vietnam, it was the same 7th Cavalry; however, instead of horses as the primary method of transportation to battle, we used helicopters, hence the attached designation "Airmobile" to our division.

After arriving at LZ Betty, we were rotated to Second Platoon of Charlie Company, and that's when I met Sgt. Jeff Porter, my platoon sergeant. After a few weeks in combat, I came to realize that Porter was Robert Mitchum, John Wayne, and Audie Murphy rolled into one. He was, without a doubt, the most fearless man I had ever met.

On the first day at LZ Betty, Sgt. Porter pulled us aside and went over things like how to pack our rucks for combat missions, correct application of camouflage on the face and hands, and, most importantly, how to keep our weapons clean while humping out in the bush.

"You won't be needing these." Porter took our heavy flak jackets and steel pots and threw them in a big pile outside the Commons area. "You guys will have enough shit to hump," he said. He handed out camouflaged Aussie bush hats and various colored camouflage sticks. "Another thing, try and stay clear of the Mad Mexican, our medic, Specialist Martinez. Don't even think of making small talk with him."

"Why is that?" Kent asked.

"Because he doesn't cotton well to cherries like you guys."

"Cherries?" Caswell asked.

Porter continued. "New guys, like you, with no combat experience. He has only sixty-five days and a wake-up before he *didis* out of this shithole, and he probably figures one of you cherries is going to 'screw the pooch' and get him killed. Also, don't even think of calling him Angel. Only me, Sgt. Roach, and a few other grunts in Charlie Company have the privilege of using that tag. When you earn his respect, well, then you can call him Angel."

Sgt. Porter relaxed, lit a Marlboro, and told us we would do just fine if we stayed alert and kept our noses clean. He mentioned that he, too, went through Tigerland at Ft. Polk, and if we remembered everything they taught us there, we had a good chance of making our DEROS date, that is, our date eligible for return from overseas in a year's time.

"And one last thing," Porter said, "don't let me catch you smoking that Black Mo in the bush. If I smell that shit, I'll be bringing the damn damn down on you so hard, you will be cursing the day you were born. Got that?"

"Got it, Sarge," we said in unison.

Chapter Seven

The Mad Mexican

"Okay, soldier, lay back and keep your mouth shut," Specialist Martinez said as he set his medic bag next to me. He elevated my head and emptied his M-5 medical kit onto a green towel he had laid out on the ground. The kit consisted of IVs, bandages, small splints, scissors, clamps, scalpels, and other items necessary for the field. He cut open my pants over the affected area, wet a clean cloth with water from his canteen, and wiped away the bloody clot on my left thigh. Missing from my upper-left thigh was a one-inch-square chunk of flesh. Blood flowed down both sides of my leg. Martinez cleaned the wound with alcohol, then applied pressure with a large bandage and told me to hold it while he searched through his kit. I felt the burn of the alcohol similar to the first moment I felt the wound. Holding the bandage in place helped.

Martinez extracted a small, silver tube with a conical plastic top that looked like the tube of cement that came with model airplane kits I had as a kid. He removed the top, revealing a long needle. Martinez squeezed the tube gently until a single drop appeared on the needle point; then he jabbed the needle into my leg, just above the open wound. I would discover later that this was a syrette of morphine.

Within seconds, I could feel the drug's intended purpose as it coursed through my veins, and felt the pain in my leg recede. A light, euphoric sensation enveloped my whole body. Minutes later, I experienced a high like nothing I had ever felt in my life. I could not feel the jungle floor beneath me. Another pleasure of the morphine was that it induced an emotional state of mind, and it made me prone to blurt out whatever random thoughts come into my head.

As Specialist Martinez dressed my wound with a large circular bandage, I asked him, "Do you think they will be able to save my leg?"

Martinez stopped what he was doing, rolled his eyes toward the sky, and shook his head. I heard him mutter something like, "Fuck, I don't even believe this shit!" He looked me square in the face and let loose. "Listen up, you DUMB CHERRY FUCK! Ain't nothing wrong with you. Probably a bark ricochet from that teak tree hit your leg. Oh, yeah. They will probably load you up on the resupply chopper coming in along with those four dead gooks. They'll take you back to the field hospital in Phan Thiêt and put a few stitches in your leg and then put your sorry ass on light duty for a few days."

It sounded good to me. Maybe I would sleep in a real bed with clean sheets for a night or two, maybe even get a hot meal. A dreamy smile crossed my face.

"But let me tell you something, Private Madigan," he added with contempt in his voice. "You're gonna hate those motherfuckin' REMFs back at Phan Thiêt."

"REMFs?" I asked.

"REAR ECHELON MOTHER FUCKERS!"

"Why's that?" I wondered why he continued to yell at me when were both right there.

"Because those fuckin' assholes know we're out here in the bush doin' all the humpin'…all the fightin'…and all the killin'. Those candy-ass pricks sit around all day crying about being in combat, writing their girlfriends bullshit stories about blowing Charlie away in the bush. That's why Ol' Charlie Viet Cong likes to send in a mortar barrage every now and then, just to let those assholes know he's watchin' their backs. And boonie rats like us put the fear of God in those pricks when we come back out of the field for a little R and R. You watch, Madigan. They won't even be able to look you straight in the eye."

"Why are you so angry, man?"

Martinez considered my question. "Because cherries like you show up in Charlie Company fresh out of Tigerland and think you're G.I 'Fuckin' Joe, man. You think your shit don't stink, and the first time you get out in the bush, you start makin' mistakes…mistakes that get people killed. I got fifty-one days and a wake-up, Private, and I don't need some dumb fucking cherry-ass soldier like you gettin' me blown away. You got that, *pendejo*?"

Martinez pulled a grease pencil out of his kit and scrawled numbers on my forehead. This was important info for the field hospital medics at the MASH unit in Phan Thiêt, detailing how much morphine had been administered.

I noticed prominent jailhouse tattoos inked on the back of his neck, a series of symbols and numbers that made no sense to me—the secret language of a violent culture back in The World. I remembered Sgt. Porter telling Caswell and me that Martinez was saved at the last minute by a sympathetic social worker from doing a three-year stint in jail. He grew up in a gang-infested neighborhood east of downtown Los Angeles called Boyle Heights. He was about to do time for grand theft larceny when his social worker convinced a judge that Angelo Martinez would be far more valuable in the Army serving his country rather than rotting in prison. The judge agreed, and Martinez signed up the next day, his eighteenth birthday.

Martinez lined up his instruments and bandages on the towel. "And Private Madigan, don't let me hear you puttin' in for a heart, fucker. Ain't no one in this outfit gets a heart till he sees the elephant, till he goes toe-to-toe and eye-to-eye with the yellow man. I hear you puttin' in for a heart, I'll make sure get one, asshole. They'll be taggin' and baggin' your ass and sending you home in a pine box with your Purple 'Fuckin' Heart.'"

My head felt light as a second wave of morphine euphoria scrambled my brain. Martinez's words seemed to jumble together and I felt as if my body had levitated off the jungle floor. My thoughts zeroed in on one of his words. *Gee,* I thought, *I didn't know there were elephants in the Nam. I thought they were only in India and Africa.* Six weeks later when Charlie Company walked into that ambush, I realized what Martinez meant about "seeing the elephant."

Assured that he had everything together, Martinez stuffed his medical instruments back into his kit. He sent Caswell to round up a few soldiers to carry me to the resupply Dust Off site.

I managed to focus and called out as the men walked away. "Hey, Specialist Martinez!"

He turned and gave me a withering stare.

"Thanks for patching me up, man."

Martinez stared at me for a few more seconds and then walked off, shaking his head and mumbling in Spanish.

Chapter Eight

Nurse Catherine

A light breeze picked up in the afternoon, and I could see whitecaps forming in the Bay of Tokyo. Once again I looked out over the Boso Peninsula to the Pacific Ocean and stared at that line on the horizon. In a moment of glory, rays of sunlight filtered down from a bank of clouds and lit the horizon with a silvery cast for miles on end. I felt as if God was communicating with me by showing me this dazzling feat of nature, a silver pathway showing me the direction home.

I heard women's laughter coming from the direction of Kishine Barracks. Looking down the pathway, I noticed two Air Force nurses draw near, strolling arm in arm, chuckling over the story they were sharing. Then my heart skipped a beat; one of the nurses was Lt. Catherine Russell, my physical therapist. I stood and greeted them.

"Oh, my!" Lt. Russell said. "Private Madigan. What a surprise."

They saw my stained pj's and it was obvious what they thought.

"Oh, these old things," I laughed as I modeled my filthy attire. "Allow me to explain." I related my extraordinary morning with Sgt. Brooks that generated nods of understanding, and told them I would be departing Japan at 2100 hours.

"Private Madigan," Catherine said, "I would like to introduce you to my friend and roommate, Lt. Anne Bennett. Anne works mostly at

Tachikawa, but she had an appointment at the 106th this afternoon. We were on our way to the Officers' Club to have coffee."

I could tell by the look on Catherine's face and her nervous voice that she thought I might slip up and signal to Anne that something wonderful happened between us, something so beautiful and unexpected that I still had a hard time believing it occurred.

I smiled and said, "Well, I would love to join you fine officers, but I don't think I'm dressed for the occasion."

Lt. Russell hesitated before speaking, "Anne, go ahead without me. I would like to talk to Private Madigan for a few moments about his condition and maybe recommend further therapy at Travis Air Force Base. I'll join you in ten minutes."

Lt. Bennett was not fooled for a second. Maybe she picked up on my face glowing with pleasure. She gave me a long look and gave Catherine a knowing grin. "Yeah, sure, Catherine. I'll see you at the club."

"Would you care to join me on my bench, Lieutenant? This is my favorite spot on the compound."

Catherine sat next to me, looked to her right and left, and when she was sure we were alone, she leaned forward for a hug and kissed me on the cheek. My day got better.

"God, Walt, I'm overjoyed at the news that you're going back to the States. I happen to know that all of you macho Air Cav guys like to pretend your wounds are no big thing. And even though yours was a flesh wound, and a large one at that, it's still a serious injury, and needs time and therapy to heal properly."

Ever the hard-assed boonie rat, I gave Catherine a dismissive wave. "I betcha' within a month of returning to California, I'll be back surfing Venice Beach."

"I have some good news, too, Walt. Next week I'll be joining Brandon in Hawaii. He finally managed to wrangle a ten-day R and R."

"Gee, that's great, Catherine," I said. I wasn't sure she could detect the twinge of disappointment in my throat.

"Um, listen, Walt, I wanted to talk to you about the night you came to my bungalow for dinner—"

"Catherine, you don't have to say another word. What happened that evening was totally unexpected on both our parts. I mean, it just happened, and it was a beautiful experience, at least for me. It was easily the best night of my life, just like today is the best day of my life. So let's leave it at that. By the time your flight arrives in Hawaii next week, you'll forget all about me and will be anxious to be with your husband."

Tears welled up in her eyes. Once again she looked around to see if the coast was clear. She hugged me and this time kissed me hard on the lips. "Thanks, Walt. I really mean that."

Lt. Catherine Russell was probably the most beautiful, intelligent, and kindest woman I had met in my short nineteen years of life. She had the appearance of what we Madigans called Black Irish: faired-skinned with thick black hair accentuated by a widows peak, a prominent forehead with long black eyebrows, blue-gray eyes, a nose as straight as a ruler with a splash of freckles, high cheekbones, and full lips that were usually smiling. I would do anything to kiss those lips.

Chapter Nine

An Invitation

I remembered my heart skipping a notch the first time I met Lt. Catherine Russell at the hospital ward in Tachikawa.

When she smiled, I noticed a small, imperceptible chip at the bottom of her right front tooth, a minor defect that offset all that beauty and gave her a much younger appearance than her twenty-three years. She stood at five feet eight and had a slender athletic figure. I was not surprised to learn she ran track in high school and college.

Catherine met her husband, Brandon, while attending the University of Wisconsin. He was on a football scholarship and signed on for ROTC during his four-year stint. Catherine graduated with a degree in nursing and attended a two-year post graduate program in physical therapy.

Then the Vietnam War changed everything. Out of college for one year and freshly married, Brandon was on the verge of getting drafted when he signed up for OTC (Officers' Training Corps), and that is how he ended up a grunt lieutenant with the Big Red One, the first division to be deployed in Vietnam.

Lt. Russell reminded me of those rich Catholic girls who would descend from their Hollywood or Beverly Hills homes on Friday night and grace us with their presence as they attended our high school sock hops. St. John Vianney was a small Catholic, all-male college preparatory institution with some tough Dominican priests running the show. We had to wear white shirts and ties on a daily basis. After eight years of being tortured by nuns in grade school (of course, I tortured them back), I was in for an even tougher time at Vianney.

Girls like Catherine displayed polite manners at the dances, but would usually decline if you asked for a dance. They were busy checking out the inventory, that being the kids of celebrities who were enrolled there. Bob Hope's son, Kelly, was in my 1965 graduating class. Loretta Young was president of the Mothers' Club and her son was one grade above me.

I didn't play traditional sports in high school, but by my junior year, I had become a pretty good surfer. I felt more confident about myself, and to my amazement, some of these young debutantes would ask *me* to dance. My problem was that once I had a girlfriend, I would soon get bored and would try to reach a little higher to grasp the girl who was a short wishing distance out of my league.

. . .

Sitting on the bench looking out at the sea, my mind wandered a few weeks back to a particular Friday afternoon when I attended my final physical therapy session with Lt. Catherine Russell. We had coffee afterwards at the nearby canteen while she reviewed my evaluation. I didn't want to think my therapy and thus my visits with her had come to an end.

"Listen, Private Madigan, my roommate is spending the weekend with her boyfriend in Tokyo, and, well, I thought it would be nice if you could come to my home tomorrow evening for a nice home-cooked meal."

Blood drained from my face and I thought I was going to faint with joy. Simply put, I was infatuated with this beautiful woman from head to toe, and her invitation put me in near shock.

"I live a mile off base, in an area of small bungalows for female Army and Air Force nurses," she said. "Here's my address. Please, be discreet about this. As you know, I could get in a lot of hot water. Say, about 7:00 p.m.?"

"I'll be there, Lieutenant. Should I bring anything?"

"Well, I'm a pretty good cook with Italian food, so why don't you pick up a bottle of Chianti at the commissary."

"Will do, Ma'am," I said in my excitement.

Chapter Ten

English Lavender

On Saturday, my first mission was to go to the commissary on base and buy some civvies for my date with Catherine. Specialist Green went with me and helped me pick out a pair of olive green Haggar slacks, a tan, short-sleeved, button-down Arrow shirt, and a plain black belt.

I had not received a paycheck from the Army since early April. My mother had sent me a cashier's check for seventy-five dollars, and Green often paid my bar bills at the NCO club at Kishine. He came from a wealthy family in Ithaca, New York. I didn't have much cash.

"Allow me to buy the Chianti, Madigan, for your big date." Green picked up two bottles before we left the commissary. He lent me a pair of maroon penny loafers and also a blue windbreaker with "Cornell" emblazoned on the back in yellow capital letters. His older brother, James, attended that prestigious university. Green handed me his bottle of Jade East cologne. "Splash a little of this on. Women love it."

I arrived at Catherine's bungalow at 7:15 p.m., getting a ride down the hill with two enlisted men from Kishine Barracks on their way to the downtown Ginza district of Tokyo where they planned to hit the bars and party for the night. When Lt. Russell opened the door, I did a double take. I had never seen her with her hair down, and it fell a little past her shoulders. She had on simple black flats, a knee-length, navy-blue pleated skirt, and a pink cardigan. A single strand of pearls adorned her neck. The top button of her sweater was undone, and I caught a glimpse of a black bra underneath.

"Oh, gee, I'm sorry," I said as I stood in the doorway trembling with excitement. "You must be Anne, Lt. Russell's roommate. She told me all about you. By the way, is Lt. Russell available?"

Catherine laughed and tugged on my arm. "Oh, get in here, silly, before anyone sees you." Once I was inside, she leaned into me and gave me a hug and a little brush on the cheek. I caught a whiff of her perfume and the fragrance seemed familiar.

"Is that lavender?" I asked.

"Yes, it is. Yardley's English Lavender. How did you know?"

"It's the only perfume my mother will wear. She seems to be allergic to other fragrances."

"Well, she has good taste. Both my mother and grandmother have been wearing English Lavender for years. My mother will even spray a little on the sheets when she changes the linens."

I didn't think Catherine could be any more beautiful, but she was tonight, wearing a little makeup, a hint of eye shadow, and a light pink gloss on her lips.

Her modest bungalow was furnished with a few stuffed chairs and a small sofa, next to which sat a tiny end table with a multi-colored Tiffany-style lamp that cast a soft, warm glow and gave the room a comfortable ambience. Japanese prints hung on the walls. She had a small stereo in the corner with about twenty or thirty albums stacked against the wall in two rows. The entire room was redolent with the smell of garlic and chicken. We moved to the kitchen where she sautéed vegetables in a skillet, and I noticed she had a wine goblet on the counter with a few sips missing.

"Wow, it smells delicious in here, Catherine."

"Good. I hope you are hungry. I've cooked enough food to feed six people. It's a chicken Parmesan recipe handed down from my grandma. I like to spice it up with lots of garlic, Italian herbs, basil and bay leaves, and, of course, lots and lots of mozzarella cheese."

"Yes, I'm hungry and getting more hungry by the minute."

"Then why don't you grab a wine glass and crack open one of those bottles of Chianti? And would you be a darling and put an album on the stereo?"

Yes, I would be a darling, I thought. *I would do a hundred pushups if she so desired.*

Catherine's taste in music was a mixed bag: opera tunes from Mario Lanza, the Ray Conniff Singers' *Somebody Loves Me*, and classical music with symphonies from Bach, Mozart and Vivaldi. Then I got to the good stuff: the Doors debut album, *Pet Sounds* by the Beach Boys, *Blonde on Blonde* by Bob Dylan, *Surrealistic Pillow* by the Jefferson Airplane, *Revolver* and *Rubber Soul* by the Beatles, and *Beggar's Banquet* by the Rolling Stones. I put on the Mamas and Papas and became a little sentimental as they began to sing: "All the leaves are gone…and the sky is gray…,"

"Good choice, Walt. I love that song. Does 'California Dreaming' make you homesick for LA?"

"More than you will ever know," I lamented.

"Dinner is ready. Take a seat in the little kitchen nook and I will fix you a plate."

The kitchen was indeed tiny. Across from the stove, the nook had enough room for a small table and two chairs.

"Hey, Catherine," I said. "I have great idea. Why don't you wrap everything up in foil, put it in the fridge, and we can go to the mess hall at Kishine and maybe catch a late meal."

Catherine almost laughed at my weak attempt at humor. Then she shot me a mock frown. "Would you just sit down, Private Madigan, and refrain from the jokes?"

"Sorry, L-T. I thought it was pretty funny."

Catherine changed the record on the stereo to Bach, and we dined to the pleasant sounds of Brandenburg Concerto No. 3 Allegro.

After dinner I helped Catherine with the dishes and tidied up the kitchen. She refilled our wine glasses, lit a few candles, dimmed the lamp, and put Paul Butterfield on the stereo. We settled on the living room sofa, listening to blues, drinking wine, and telling stories of our past.

Our backgrounds could not have been more different. Catherine was the eldest of three girls and grew up on the picturesque shores of Lake Geneva, Wisconsin. Her father, an architect, designed second homes for a wealthy clientele from the metropolitan areas of Milwaukee and nearby Chicago. Her mother was an elementary school teacher who taught close to their home. Both parents were avid outdoors people, and Catherine's summers were filled with activities, such as camping, fishing, canoeing, and sailing on Lake Geneva. She braved bitter cold winters to go cross-country skiing and ice-skating on smaller lakes near her home. Lake Geneva, with a population under seven thousand, was dubbed "Newport of the West" in reference to Newport, Rhode Island.

By contrast, I grew up on the West Coast in the urban sprawl of Los Angeles, California. By the time I was thirteen in 1960, the population had risen to two and a half million. I was number six of eight children and came from a blue-collar, working-class, Irish Catholic family. My father never finished high school and worked long hours as a switchman/brakeman for the Southern Pacific Railroad in downtown LA. We lived in a small Spanish-style stucco house that my father had originally purchased for his mother and him in the early 1930s.

"How did your parents meet?" Catherine asked.

"Well, you see my mother, Nellie, met and married a man in her hometown of Omaha, Nebraska, when she was twenty-two and soon they had a daughter, my half-sister, Virginia, who was born in 1935. Nellie's husband, Arley Jones, turned out to be a real cad and one day announced, 'Nellie, you have been a real queen, but I can't handle the responsibility of marriage and being a father.' And just like that, he abandoned my mother and his daughter, and took off for parts unknown. I'm sure it was more complicated than that, but all the same, he took off into thin air and left my poor mother crushed and brokenhearted. My half-sister, whom we nicknamed 'Dee Dee,' once told me how madly in love my mother was with this guy."

Catherine let this information sink in. "Oh, Walt, that is so sad. How did she meet your father?"

"So my mother decided to pack it up and she left Omaha with her daughter in tow. Nellie's mom died shortly after Nellie was born in 1913 from some sort of complication as a result of the birth, which was not uncommon in those days. Since she didn't have the option of going home to Mother, she went to live with her cousin, Mary, and Aunt Ma. Ma was my mother's aunt. They lived in Southern California."

Catherine took another sip of wine. "Tell me more."

"All right. My mother managed to get a job in downtown Los Angeles with Pacific Telephone and Telegraph. She worked in the telegraph department and can you believe it? She actually wore roller skates to speed up delivery between her desk and the telephone operators."

"That's fascinating. Go on."

"At her job, my mother became friends with a woman named Cecilia who had moved in with her brother in Los Angeles. My mom and Cecilia became best friends. They both loved to dance and would often go to dance clubs on Olympic Boulevard near downtown LA.

In those days, swing music was the big thing with large orchestras providing the tunes."

"Like Tommy Dorsey?"

"Exactly. So one night Cecilia decided to bring her brother, Cornelius, to a dance hall where she was to meet up with my mother."

"I think I know where this is heading."

"Yep. My father had never married, worked long hours with the railroad, and was a bit shy when it came to meeting women. He could be a dapper dresser, and liked to dance to Big Band music. For some reason, Cecilia had a feeling that Nellie and Cornelius would get along, and, well, they did get along. They fell madly in love and got hitched. My mother had seven more children. I was sixth in line, including Dee Dee."

"That makes eight kids in all," Catherine said. "How old was your father when he married your mother?"

I had to think about her question. "You're not going to believe this, Lieutenant. My father was born in St. Louis in 1890. His parents, my direct grandparents, were breathing when Lincoln was still alive."

"Abraham Lincoln?" she said. Her eyes widened and her mouth stayed agape.

"Yep. My grandparents were born in 1863 and '64. Lincoln was assassinated in '65. They were only babies, but breathing when Lincoln was still alive. I believe my parents married in 1937. My mother was twenty-four, and my dad would have been…forty-seven. Their first arrival, my eldest brother, Neal, that's a shortened version of Cornelius, was born in 1940. There's William, who we called Kelly, that's his middle name. My sister, Kathleen, my sister, Maureen, me, my younger brother, James, and sister, Helen."

"Is your father still alive?"

"No. He died in 1963. He was 72."

"I'm sorry, Walt," she said. "On the other hand, your mother must be thrilled that you are safe and recovering here in Japan."

"Yeah. She's relieved that I'm currently out of the war zone, but she won't be happy to know I'm recovering so well—thanks to you, LT—because that means they'll send me back to my unit in Vietnam sooner rather than later.

"I used to beg and plead for one more hour. 'Please, Dad, *pretty please*!' " I acted the part and Catherine laughed. "But he would always say, 'An hour is enough. Why don't you learn to bodysurf the waves and you won't need a raft?'

"And you know what, Lieutenant? I did. I'd bob around in the water and learned the rhythm and rotation of waves, how they would roll in and break in sets. I discovered that the third or fourth wave in a set was usually the biggest, the most well-formed, and provided the longest ride."

"That's great, Walt," she said. "When did you get your first surfboard?"

"Okay, so my best friend, Greg Ross, turned sixteen in January of '63 and his dad, who was a landscaper, gave him his old work truck, a 1947 Ford panel truck. Greg had his license and the timing could not have been better. I mean, *geez*, it was the perfect surf wagon and we were determined to learn how to surf so we could be…well, cool, and pick up all the hot surfer girls who mostly hung out on the shore. The whole surf scene was just beginning. We'd have the Beach Boys' 'Surfin' Safari' blaring on the radio. We were getting in on the ground floor, if you will.

"Greg and I were sophomores in '63, and every morning in February he would swing by my house around 5:45 to pick me up, and sometimes he brought his friend, Paul Matyas. We liked this one beach about three miles north of the pier that had a lighthouse and two jetties."

"Did you wear wetsuits? The water had to be really cold that time of the year."

"Wetsuits! Are you kidding? I could barely afford my first surfboard. I got a Con, made by a man named Con Colburn from his shop on Pico Boulevard in Santa Monica. And, yes, the water was freezing, but we were so determined to learn how to surf, we toughed it out. And you know what? By June, we were pretty decent surfers, unlike the gremmies who dressed like surfers, but never ventured offshore."

"Gremmies?" she laughed.

"Yeah, guys who dressed like surfers and even lightened their hair with lemon juice, but didn't know a surfboard from a closet door. I guess you could call them 'pretend surfers.' Then we formed a club called Hoshi Surf Club."

"Hoshi? That's an odd name," Catherine said.

"That beach I mentioned with the lighthouse and two jetties; we discovered that the second jetty north of the lighthouse had the best break and more consistent waves, but for some reason, it was called the Horseshit Jetty by the locals. We were good Catholic high school boys, L-T. We couldn't call ourselves the Horseshit Surf Club or say it in front of our parents. We shortened it to Hoshi."

"Yeah. But you knew even if your parents didn't."

She laughed and then I laughed. The drink was doing its job.

"Oh! Oh!" She sat up. "You have to know this. There's a line in one of those Beach Boys' songs about a dance." She sang the words she could remember. " '...something, the surf is down, something... and we'll do the Surfer Stomp, the latest dance craze.' Pray tell, what is the Surfer Stomp?"

"Oh, come on, Catherine. You've never heard of the Surfer Stomp?"

"I've heard of it, but the dance never made it to the shores of Lake Geneva."

"Hah! Guess what? You're in for a treat because I'm going to teach you the Surfer Stomp, right here, right now." I got off the sofa and flipped through her albums.

"I think I have a Dick Dale album. Will that do?"

"Perfect!" I said.

I found the album, put it on the turntable and turned up the volume. Her bungalow filled with the burning single string staccato of "Miserlou."

I reached for Catherine's hand.

"Uh, I don't think so," Catherine said.

"I'm not going to show you. You're going to do it with me."

I pulled Catherine up off the sofa and had her stand facing me. I backed up about two feet, and said, "Now put your feet slightly apart and watch me." I snapped my fingers, slid my right foot back, then forward and stomped. Then I repeated the move with my left foot, slid it back, then forward and stomped.

Catherine brought her palms up to her face and laughed hysterically. "Oh, my God. That's the silliest dance I've ever seen. You look like a caveman trying to stomp out a fire."

"You wouldn't be saying that if you were at the Rendezvous Ballroom in Balboa Beach on a Friday night with six hundred surfer dudes and girls all doing the stomp to Dick Dale and his Del-Tones. Man, it was some sight to see. Come on, Catherine, give it a shot."

I restarted "Miserlou" and began to dance. Catherine tried to follow, but she was even more tipsy from the second bottle of wine, and it didn't help that she could not stop laughing. She stepped forward, leaned in and put her arms around my neck.

"Walt, this is so much fun. I really needed a night like this. Thank you so much for coming over."

"My pleasure, Catherine."

Then she leaned in further, put her head on my shoulder and gave me a long warm kiss on my neck. We stood locked together for several seconds swaying back and forth to the music. She began to tremble, and I heard small muffled whimpers.

Oh, Jesus, I thought. *She's crying.* At that moment I wanted to put my lips against hers, press her close to me and make love to her right there in the living room. But, alas, my better angels kicked in, and I heard a small voice in the back of my head: *Cool your jets, cowboy. She's a little drunk and is probably thinking about Brandon. Whatever you do, DO NOT take advantage of the situation. Be a good guy and let things play out.*

"Gee, Catherine, maybe I should be getting on back to Kishine."

She backed up and gazed at me with her beautiful smoky blue-gray eyes. A little mascara streaked down her cheek. "No, not yet, Walt. Could you please stay a little longer? I just had a moment there, but I'm fine. Please don't go yet."

I sat back down on the sofa as Catherine went to freshen up in the bathroom. When she came out, she seemed composed, put Dylan on the stereo and joined me on the couch.

"Listen L-T, I've been painting a pretty rosy picture of what it was like to be a surfer during high school. I mean it was great and all that, but there's another whole side I didn't mention—a very dark side."

She perked up hearing this intrigue. "Really, Walt? What would that be?"

"Well, you see," I said, "being a surfer in Los Angeles meant that you invariably had a natural predator."

"Like sharks?"

"Well, yes, we had to be on the lookout for sharks; however, I'm talking about a subgroup of mammals: hodads." I said with the seriousness of a monsignor delivering a eulogy.

"Okay, I give up." Catherine laughed, seeing through my fake veneer. "Pray tell, what is a hodad?"

"A hodad is a greaser, a punk, a guy who still uses pomade in his hair to make a pompadour. The ones who wear black leather jackets, white T-shirts, and cuffed jeans. You know, like those guys in the movie, *The Wild One,* with Brando. Those guys are into loud machines, motorcycles and souped-up cars, not surfboards."

"Weren't your older brothers like that? I think you told me that they were into car clubs."

"That's true. Kelly was in a club called Trophy Bandits and Neal was in a smaller club called Slo-Pokes. But keep in mind, the whole surf craze in Southern California hadn't begun yet. It was the mid- to late-fifties, and car clubs were still the thing. Being a hodad was the norm during those times.

"One time, my best friend, Fred Benoit, and I snuck out of my parents' house at one o' clock in the morning to go down to Venice Boulevard. We watched the Trophy Bandits barricade the street with sawhorses they stole from a nearby construction site so they could drag race other car clubs. And remember Natalie Wood in *Rebel Without a Cause?* The hottest looking Trophy Bandit girlfriend would be out there in the middle island of the boulevard holding up a scarf as two muscle cars revved their engines on either side of her. When she dropped the scarf, all you heard were tires screaming, and engines roaring, and we would be choking on a plume of exhaust as the cars took off and raced to the finish line at Thurman Avenue."

"Wow, I feel like I've lived on another planet compared to you. I never experienced any of that growing up in Lake Geneva."

"And I kind of got sidetracked," I said. "I wanted you to get a feeling for what a hodad was all about. Now I'm going to tell you about a night seared in my memory like none other, an evening I'll never forget as long as I live," I said with all the solemnity I could muster.

"Ooh! Hold that thought. "Catherine jumped off the sofa and ran to the kitchen. "I want to settle in and hear all about your evening of infamy. First, have you ever tasted liebfraumilch?"

"Sounds German, L-T. What is it?"

"It's a sweet German white wine. My roommate is going to kill me for opening her bottle of Blue Nun, but what the hell."

"I don't know, L-T. Do you think we should still be drinking at this late hour? As it is, I'm going to have a hard enough time finding my way back to Kishine Barracks.

"Listen, Walt, you're not going back to Kishine. You can crash on my couch until morning and sneak out of here before daylight. I'm having way too much fun, and you are not going anywhere, Private First Class Madigan. I don't want to think about tomorrow, or even an hour from now. I only want to stay in the moment and hear your dark tale about hodads. I do outrank you, Private, and that's an order!"

"If you say so, Lieutenant," I gave her a mock salute.

Catherine filled two wine glasses and joined me on the sofa. She raised her glass and said, "*Salute*," and before I could take a sip, she leaned into me and gave me a peck on the lips.

Chapter Twelve

Surf Gods

I sipped the sweet German wine Catherine handed me. "Before I get to our encounter with the hodads, I need to tell you about a surfing adventure that took place earlier that day, because what happened ties in with our confrontation with the greasers later that evening."

"Okay."

Catherine snuggled closer to me on the sofa and sipped her wine. I noticed another button had come undone on her sweater, and it took every ounce of my self-control not to stare at her lacy black bra. I started in on the story.

My junior class sat for First Friday Mass in the chapel attached to my high school, St. John Vianney. The day had been unseasonably hot in Los Angeles for early March, and we perspired in our required uniforms: dark blazers, white shirts, tie, and ironed slacks. After listening to a grueling sermon by our principal, Father Vincent Cavalli, and reciting prayers for the Stations of the Cross, we were mercifully cut loose for the rest of the weekend.

I rushed home to call my best friend, Greg Ross. Greg and his schoolmate, Paul Matyas, attended St. Bernard by the beach in Playa del Rey. They had a short Friday too. I knew there was a storm brewing down in Baja, Mexico, which meant the waves would be good at Sunset, our new surf spot. The beach was aptly named since it was located where Sunset Boulevard wound down from the Pacific Palisades and dead-ended into Pacific Coast Highway, or as we called it, PCH.

Sunset Beach was a rocky point facing southwest, and often the waves sectioned off in a southerly direction to smaller breaks. With luck, a surfer could catch a ride that lasted several minutes, and if there was the slightest weather disturbance south of the border, you could count on a good lineup of three- and four-foot waves, sometimes higher.

Greg came by my house at 2:45 p.m. I loaded my surfboard into the back of his panel truck. Greg removed the two small rear windows on the back doors so we could slide two boards through the openings and fasten a rope around the rear fins. I threw in a few towels, a fresh T-shirt, suntan lotion, and a pair of shorts for *après* surf. Next stop was Paul's house. Paul lived close to Helm's Bakery on a side street off Venice Boulevard. After he loaded his board, we set off for our afternoon surfing adventure.

Sunset Beach was pure glass with no offshore breeze. Incoming swells caught the sparkle of the late afternoon sun, which glistened on the walls of water like a million tiny diamonds. Sets arrived at three and four feet with an occasional five-footer breaking off the point from left to right.

Two of Paul's friends from grammar school, Dave Foch and Jim Fischer, met up with us on the low cliffs where Greg parked his truck. We walked down the path to the beach, and spent several minutes on the shore waxing our boards and planning a strategy.

"COWABUNGA!" Greg screamed as he threw his board in the ocean and began paddling like crazy toward the first set of breakers. Paul, Dave, Jim, and I followed as we made our way out to the rocky point. There were at least three dozen surfers in the water, but only five or six straddling their boards on the northernmost point.

Sitting there, parked on my surfboard in between sets, I could see all the surf wagons dotting PCH: woodies, pickup trucks, modified VW buses, panel trucks like Greg's, and several brightly painted station wagons. Beyond the highway the taller cliffs of Pacific Palisades made way for beautiful homes on large lots of land with sensational views of the boundless blue Pacific Ocean.

Every few years after a particularly long and wet winter, a large mansion would teeter on the precipice of the steep, eroding cliffs. In time the cliff would give way, or the weight of the overhanging house would succumb to gravity, sending it crashing down onto the middle of PCH where it would come to rest like a giant beached whale.

Greg was easily the most athletic of our group, and he seemed to catch waves with slight effort. He was a star athlete at St. Bernard and began playing varsity basketball as a sophomore. He was also an A student and often had a beautiful girl wrapped around his arm at parties and high school dances. However, it was Paul, not Greg, who caught the best ride that day.

I was paddling back out to the point after a long ride when I heard a surfer yell, "OUTSIDE!" Just beyond the last set was a large, fast-moving swell at least six feet high that rose out of nowhere.

Paul was in perfect position at the point with two other surfers, both of whom turned and caught the last wave of the earlier set. This left Paul in good position for the rogue wave, which gained momentum as it rolled in his direction. Paul turned his board toward shore at the last second and barely took a stroke or two as the swell picked up the tail of his surfboard. He waited until his board was halfway up the face, jumped to his feet and took off with his right foot forward, his left foot back, and his backside to the wave in what we called riding goofy-foot.

I sat on my board, slack-jawed. I had never seen Paul attempt this stance before. The crest of the large wave began to curl from left to right as Paul sped down the face and executed a perfect bottom turn. He used his speed and momentum to climb back up the face and fire on down the line.

Then, inexplicably, the wave began to stall. I thought Paul would step back on his board and ride up the face to kick out over the crest before he went over the falls, that is, before getting caught up in the wave after losing his board, but Paul had something else in mind. He took a few steps forward and went into a crouch and grabbed the outside rail of his board with his left hand. As the wave began to form into a barrel, Paul went into a low tuck and disappeared into the wormhole. He became invisible for several seconds as the wave continued to curl left to right instead of closing out. At the last second, Paul shot out of the southernmost point of the wave, a gust of sea mist and foamy white soup fast on his heels. Then he stepped back a foot or two, arched his back, and rode up to the crest for a spectacular kick out as the wave closed behind him.

"Holy shit, Paul!" I muttered to myself, having seen one hell of a ride.

Lots of whistles, hoots and hollers came forth from the surfers who witnessed Paul's amazing feat. Horns honked up on PCH.

When the occasion called for it at the end of our day, we would perform a ritual called King of the Surf Gods. This day, and indeed, this surfer, merited a ceremony. Paul sat beaming on a large rock as Greg made a wreath out of seaweed. Dave, Jim, and I gathered in a semicircle and knelt in the sand as if we were in church. Greg approached and instructed Paul to kneel down on one knee, and like King

Arthur knighting Lancelot, he placed the wreath on Paul's head. "Hail, Paul Matyas!" he shouted for all to hear. "King of the Surf Gods!"

We echoed Greg's pronouncement and in a show of deference, threw our arms over our heads and down toward the sand, back and forth, bowing to our king.

"There you have it, L-T, the first part of the story, Give me a break and I'll tell you the second half, if you're still want to hear it."

"You bet I do. I told you, I don't care how late it gets."

After a bathroom break, I continued my tale.

Greg dropped me off at six and said he would come back to pick me up. At eight, he and I and Paul had planned to go to the YMCA in Hollywood for the weekly Friday night dance. A local surf band would be providing the entertainment.

Before jumping in the shower, I laid out a wardrobe on my bed: a new wool Pendleton shirt with hues of blue, red, and gray; chocolate brown wide-wale corduroy trousers; a crisp white, wide-collar JCPenney Towncraft T-shirt; white socks, and a pair of tan leather huarache sandals I picked up two weeks earlier in Tijuana, Mexico.

Maureen, who was now a freshman in college and studying theater arts, was getting ready for her own date. She knocked on my bedroom door as I was splashing on Aqua Velva and came into my room to check out my attire for the evening. I told her about our afternoon surfing adventure at Sunset Beach and about Paul's coronation as King of the Surf Gods.

Maureen, along with my younger sister, Helen, absolutely adored Paul. Maureen made sure I invited him to her frequent theater parties. Paul, Greg, and I loved those events as we would gawk at her beautiful girlfriends who were often auditioning for plays, small parts in movies, and TV commercials. Three years later, Maureen would audition for a Ford Mustang commercial and win the part. Maureen once told me she would have snatched up Paul in a second if he were only a few years older.

Greg showed up on time, wearing a Pendleton shirt, a white T-shirt, dark blue Levis, no socks, and a pair of sandals that looked as though he had borrowed them from Mahatma Gandhi. He also donned his new rimless granny glasses, which were coming into vogue.

Paul prided himself on being a snappy dresser and was wearing slightly wrinkled tan chinos, black-and-white Converse tennis shoes, a multi-colored madras shirt, and a lightweight green cotton jacket. Maureen came into the living room and falling to her knees said, "Hail Paul Matyas! King of the Surf Gods!" Greg and I cracked up as Maureen walked up to Paul, gave him a big hug and kissed him on the cheek.

"Ooh, Paul," she exclaimed. "You are so damn handsome, you make my heart swoon!"

"Okay, come on guys," I said. "Let's get the hell out of here before Paul's head swells to the size of a watermelon."

The gym at the YMCA substituted as a dance hall on Friday nights, and surfers of all stripes were making the scene. Soon we ran into Dave Foch and Jim Fischer and other former members of the now defunct Hoshi Surf Club. Our main topic of conversation was the glorious afternoon we spent at Sunset Beach.

"Tasty waves, guys," Dave said. "And Paul, you were amazing. When did you learn to take off goofy-footed?"

"To tell you the truth," Paul said, "it was my first time to attempt that stance on a wave. I used to practice getting up off my board goofy-footed in the sand, but when I saw that giant swell heading my way, I thought now is as good a time as ever. By the way, Dave, I was scared shitless. It's always risky taking off at the point, and if I wiped out, my board would have ended up on the rocks."

The local surf band was decent and as the night wore on, the gym filled to the rafters as teens began to twist, shake, and shimmy to the rock music. Some did the Watusi, others the Frug, and a group of girls next to us were trying out the latest dance fad, the Pony.

Dave, Jim, and I walked over to the girls doing the Pony and invited them to join our circle. Then the band went into their own version of "Pipeline" by the Chantays, and the crowd went wild. Soon there was nothing but a sea of writhing bodies as our group began to Surfer Stomp. We taught the Pony girls how to Stomp and the night ended with sore feet, sweaty brows, and tired grins.

Chapter Thirteen

Greasers and Glasspacks

"What a story, Walt," Catherine said. "I loved the part about Paul dropping into the wave goofy-footed and then getting swallowed up into the wormhole. And your night at the YMCA with the Pony girls. I've heard of the Watusi, but not the Frug. I wonder if those girls laughed as hard as I did when you tried to teach them the Surfer Stomp."

I feigned a moue.

"All right," Catherine said, "so when am I going to hear about the hodads?"

"Patience, L-T," I said. "First, I wanted you to get a sense of what our day was like before we encountered our natural predators—the hodads."

"Now this is a three-part story."

"Yep. Here's what went down."

It was close to 11:30 p.m. when we left the YMCA and decided to cruise the A&W Drive-In on the corner of Venice Boulevard and Sepulveda. This was a popular hangout on Friday nights for the surf crowd from Venice, Santa Monica, and State Beach. Greg had installed a tiny two-seat couch in the rear of the panel truck where I rode in comfort; it was Paul's turn to ride shotgun in front. Paul had left his surfboard in the truck, and we decided to place it through one of the rear window slits with the skeg of the board resting on the back door so I would have more legroom.

"Besides," I said, "in case the babes don't get it that this is a surf wagon, the skeg hanging out should do the trick."

A&W was packed as usual, but we managed to find a spot about four spots down from the restaurant service door. Like a drive-in theater, there was a pole and speaker planted off the driver's side door. Greg pushed the button to order burgers, fries, and mugs of their famous root beer for the three of us. Fifteen minutes later our waitress approached, balancing a platter of food above her head and carrying a tray that would attach to the side of Greg's window.

As we gulped down our burgers and fries, I heard a loud rumble outside and the panel truck began to shake. At first I thought we were experiencing an earthquake. Paul looked out his window to the right, and muttered, "Oh, geez, we got greaseballs at three o' clock."

I leaned forward from the back and looked over Paul's shoulder to see a 1957 Ford Skyliner, the model with the retracting hardtop roof. The candy-apple-green Ford had baby moon hubcaps, and a huge chrome box-like thing protruding out of the hood.

Greg leaned forward to get a view of the Skyliner and let out a low whistle. "Holy shit," he said. "Will you look at the size of the blower on that machine? That has to house at least two carburetors, and judging from the sound of those mufflers, they have to be Cherry Bomb Glasspacks.

"Gee, Greg," I said, "You are a veritable font of information. How in the hell do you know all that?"

"I've got three older brothers, and they all had hot rods and belonged to car clubs. So I have a little knowledge of muscle cars."

"I guess that ship has sailed for us," Paul said.

"Yeah, I guess so," Greg said.

There were three hodads in the Ford, two up front and one guy in the back seat. All appeared to be in their early 20s, and all three sported slick pompadours with enough grease in their hair to lube my '56 Chevy for the next year.

The driver, who we soon found out was Frankie and the apparent leader of this trio, resembled Sal Mineo, the actor. He checked out Greg's panel truck, prompting him to sneer his ugly face, and he muttered something to his partner riding shotgun.

The guy sitting in the back was the scariest looking of the bunch. He had black, oily sidewalls plastered to the sides of his head. He had on a tight red T-shirt and looked to be at least one hundred pounds overweight. When he looked in our direction, I noticed he had a colossal block of a head, more of a snout than a nose, and his large nostrils visible along with fleshy lips. His half-lidded eyes cast a dull look on his face. In short, he resembled a frightening, giant pig.

"Man, those are three ugly dudes," Paul said.

"Just ignore them," Greg said. "They look like trouble." He took another bite of his sandwich and settled back into his seat.

A few minutes later, a shiny maroon '57 Ford Thunderbird with a white top crawled by in the lane perpendicular to our parking spot. I caught a glimpse of the girls in the two-seater, a blonde on the right, and the driver, a brunette. I also noticed a wry smile on Greg's face as his eyes followed the T-Bird down to the end of the row.

The girls made a U-turn and pulled into the vacant spot on Greg's left. The driver opened her door and stepped out. She was a raven-haired, doe-eyed beauty with milky-white skin and natural ruby-red lips, one of those rare attractive girls who needed neither makeup nor lipstick to enhance her feminine virtues. She headed to Greg's window with a little smile on her face. Greg chuckled as he watched her approach. She was wearing all black: black turtleneck, black slacks, and black flats, even her nails were painted black. She looked like a *femme fatale* off the screen of a 1940's black-and-white *film noir* movie.

"Hi, Greg," she said. She leaned into his truck and kissed him on the cheek.

"Well, well, well. Kim Greenhowe," Greg said in a joyful tone as he leaned out of his seat to kiss her on the lips.

Jesus, I thought, *how does this guy do it? I mean, this girl is drop-dead gorgeous and Greg is acting as casually as if he were talking to his sister.*

Kim and her friend, Pamela Newhouse, "Pammy" to her friends, both attended St. Bernard along with Paul and Greg. Greg had been dating Kim off and on for the past two months.

"So what are you girls up to tonight?" Greg asked.

"Oh, we just left a dull party in Westchester, lots of gremmies there. Not the real thing like you guys," Kim said.

"You got *that* right," Paul said.

"Hi, Paul."

"Hi, Kim."

Pammy stepped out of the T-Bird. Pammy was no beauty like Kim, but she was no slouch either. As Paul was often wont to say of Catholic girls at St. Bernard, "She just missed being beautiful." Standing at five feet eight, she was a tall, leggy blond with well-toned, tanned muscles. Greg told me she was the only girl he knew at St. Bernard who surfed, a rarity indeed. She was wearing a long-sleeved Madras blouse rolled up at the sleeves and tied off in a knot beneath her generous breasts, which in turn, showed off her bronzed midriff. She also wore a pair of tight-fitting white capri pants cut in a split below her knees to accentuate her tanned, well-toned calves and curvy backside. Long white-blonde tresses flowed down over her shoulders, perhaps a little too blonde with help from a bottle.

If any of the nuns or priests at St. Bernard saw her in that getup, she would have been expelled on the spot, maybe even ex-communicated from the Catholic Church. In a phrase, Pammy was the living archetype of the quintessential California surfer girl.

Pammy walked around the front of the panel truck and rested her elbows below Paul's window. I noticed all three hodads were entranced with her movements, and all three had their eyes glued to her heart-shaped ass.

"Hi, Paul." Pammy snapped her chewing gum. "Whatcha guys up to?"

"We were up in Hollywood rockin' to a pretty good surf band at the YMCA. Man, my dogs are barking."

"Your dogs are barkin' huh?" she replied as she snapped her gum even louder.

"My feet, Pammy, they're hurtin' from doing the Surfer Stomp all night."

"So, Paul, I hear you're King of the Surf Gods."

"Yeah. Where did you hear that?"

Pammy smiled and said, "A little birdie told me. Word gets around fast in Westchester."

She leaned in Paul's window and looked in back of the truck. She flashed a smile at me, her brilliant white teeth straightened from years of braces and expensive dental work. "So, who's your friend in back, Paul? I haven't seen him before. Does he go to St. Bernard?"

"That's Walt. He goes to St. John Vianney up in Hollywood with all those rich kids. Kelly Hope, Bob Hope's son, is in his junior class."

"Yeah?" Pammy said, once more snapping her gum. "Are you rich, Walt?"

"Not by any means," I said. "I'm probably the poorest kid going to that school."

Pammy smiled and said to Paul, "He's kinda cute. You should invite him to our sock hops."

No question, Pamela Newhouse was on the prowl.

Paul laughed and turned around to look at me. "Yeah," Paul said in a mocking tone, "I guess he is kinda cute."

For sitting in the back, I had a good view of the action and my eyes shifted back to the Ford Skyliner when both of its car doors opened. Frankie and his buddy riding shotgun walked forward and leaned against the left front fender of the muscle car. They continued to stare at Tammy's backside as if rudeness was a compliment.

Frankie's friend was a tall, gangly fellow with a pocked-marked complexion. Wispy hairs hung off his chin and even fewer hairs beneath his hawk-shaped nose. Frankie whispered to him, and when his friend laughed, he displayed small, discolored, pointy teeth and his black beady eyes narrowed. In a nutshell, Frankie's friend looked like the large Norway rat I had seen in a horror flick a few nights back.

Pammy turned around to check them out and after a quick once-over, turned back to Paul. "Jesus," she said. "Those guys are really creeping me out."

"Ah, you can ignore them," Paul said. "They're just loser hodads living in the past."

"Hey, Pammy," Kim yelled. "C'mon, let's order something. I'm starving."

"Okay. Paul, see you in history class on Monday." She stuck her head in the truck and flashed me another smile. "Nice meeting you, Walt."

"Yeah," I said. "Same here, Pammy."

As Pammy walked toward the front of Greg's truck, Frankie went into his best James Dean pose, lit a cigarette, and said, "Hey, doll, how about a date?"

Pammy stopped in her tracks and shook her head back and forth as if she was wondering whether she heard Frankie right. Then she turned and shot him a look of unfailing disdain. "Fuck off, loser!" She shouted loud enough for teenagers in adjoining cars to hear, and in return we heard whistles, cheers, and jeers, and a smattering of applause.

"*Cunt!*" Frankie hissed. Then he turned to Ratface and said loud enough for both girls to hear, "Do you believe that fuckin' bitch?"

"Let's split," Tammy said to Kim. "I lost my appetite."

Kim started the T-Bird as Pammy got in. Both girls ignored the hodads as they drove out of the A&W lot. I could tell Frankie was enraged from the crimson pall on his face. Both he and Ratface bent low and flipped the girls off as they drove by. Then they turned their gaze on us. Paul was still laughing about the whole incident, which enraged Frankie even more. He and Ratface raised their arms high and flipped the bird at Greg and Paul.

"Okay, guys, we're outta here." Greg flicked his headlights on and off to get the attention of our waitress. She saw Greg's signal from one spot away, and when she walked over, we all threw money at her so we could get the hell out of there.

As soon as she removed the tray and empty plates, Greg started his truck and pulled out to the right in order to hit the exit onto Sepulveda Boulevard. As we passed the Ford Skyliner, all three greasers were giving us the stink eye, and, of course, flipping us off.

And then Paul, in his inimitable style, displayed a shit-eatin' grin at Frankie, Ratface and Piggy, and decided to scratch the little area between his eyebrows…with his middle finger. I felt the blood drain from my face as I heard the familiar roar of those Cheery Bomb Glasspacks come to life.

Chapter Fourteen

The Chase

I scrambled to the back of the panel truck and peeked out one of the window slits. To my utter horror, I watched as the Ford Skyliner peeled out of its spot, trays still attached to the windows, plates and mugs of root beer flying in every direction. Frankie honked his horn and blinked his headlights, warning people to get out of the way.

"Jesus, Paul!" I screamed. "You really did it this time, man. These guys are pissed. They're going to hunt us down and go for blood."

"Fuck 'em if they can't take a joke," Paul replied, even as the Ford Skyliner was in hot pursuit of Greg's truck.

Greg drove toward Venice Boulevard and turned east in the direction of our homes. He gave it the gas and we hit sixty miles per hour on Venice.

Every time I clambered to the back and peeked out, I saw the hodads right on our tail. Greg approached a red light at Robertson Boulevard.

"Fuck it, Greg," I yelled. "Run the red light and head to my house. It's after midnight, and with any luck, my big brother will be home from his swing shift at Western Gillette."

Greg was paranoid about getting any more tickets, having received two in the last three months, and stayed put. As he waited for the light to change, Frankie started banging on Greg's side window with his fist.

"Get outta the truck, fuckers! We're going to kick your sorry asses!"

Then Ratface was at Paul's window, beating hard and screaming the same invectives. Paul, unfazed as he looked at Ratface, decided once again to scratch that little space between his eyes, and yes, with his middle finger.

I felt like I was watching a ping-pong match as I shifted my eyes from one window to the next, until I felt a rocking sensation at the back of the truck and turned around. Paul's surfboard was on the move. I peeked out and saw Piggy easing Paul's board out the back.

"*Shit!* That fat fucker is trying to steal your board, Paul."

I grabbed both rails and waited to feel a little slack; then with all my strength, I rammed the board in Piggy's direction until it stopped with a dull *thunk,* followed by a scream. I pulled in the board and peered out the window slit. Piggy held his nose and blood leaked between his fingers.

"YOU BROKE MY NOSE! YOU COCKSUCKER! YOU'RE GOING TO DIE NOW, ASSHOLE!"

"Good move, Walt," Paul said. "I owe you one." The light turned green and Greg floored it down Venice Boulevard.

Please, God, I prayed as we approached my house on Marvin Avenue, *please let Kelly be home.*

Greg had the radio on and the Beach Boy's "I Get Around" blared from the speakers, "…the bad guys know us and they leave us alone." The irony of that last line was not lost on us as we looked at each other and intoned with gallows humor, "Not tonight!"

"Man, I hope your brother is home," Greg said. "I still can't believe what he did to that guy, Tim, at Neal's party a few months back."

Greg was referring to a party my oldest brother, Neal, and his young wife, Cathy, had in celebration of their new apartment in Inglewood. They had been married one year and had a newborn, Scott, and decided to have a little Saturday night family get-together.

My older sister, Kathy, who was out of high school a few years, was a real beauty with amazing violet-colored eyes like Elizabeth Taylor. She had no trouble getting dates, and the phone rang day and night from men in pursuit, much to the dismay of my mother. Kathy's problem was an attraction to losers, and Tim, her date that night, was a real loser.

Tim had downed two or three drinks before showing up at the gathering with my sister. Kelly attended the party with his fiancée, Frances Butler, who set her radar on Kathy's date should he get out of line. By 11:00 p.m., Tim was shit-faced and had been warned twice by Kelly to keep his voice down and lay off the booze. There would be no third warning. Greg and I were hanging out on the second floor balcony sneaking a cigarette when we heard Tim blurt out to my sister and everyone else nearby, "Oh yeah, that guy. He's a real *fuckin' asshole.*"

That was it for Kelly. He stormed over to Tim, picked him up by the lapels of his jacket, and literally dragged him across the living room floor and out the front door. Before Tim had a chance to react, Kelly slammed him up against a post on the balcony and bitch-slapped him three or four times. On impulse, Kelly threw Tim down the stairs to the first floor like a bag of garbage. Fortunately for Tim, he was so drunk, he went into a soft roll until he splayed out on the landing wondering what happened.

Greg and I stood there in shock. "Jesus, Kelly," Greg said. "I guess that guy really pissed you off."

Kelly shot us a look that froze my heart. Had he not been my older brother and self-appointed *paterfamilias* of the Madigan clan since my dad passed a year earlier, I think I would have turned and run. Never in a million years could I affect a look like that—a look that would put absolute terror in a man's heart. I was born with a genteel nature much like my older brother, Neal. I liked to think of myself as a lover, not a fighter.

"Fucker should have listened to me the first time," Kelly said in disgust as he went back into the apartment to join the party.

"Okay, Walt, we're getting close to your house," Greg said, "and they're still hot on our tail. What should I do?"

Marvin Avenue, a dead-end street, T-boned into Ballona Creek, a concrete waterway offshoot of the LA river system. During intense winter storms, the creek carried excess water down into Santa Monica Bay. If Kelly wasn't home from his shift, we would be doomed to fend for ourselves.

"It's twelve-forty," I said. "He has to be home by now. Just go for it."

Greg turned right on Marvin and the hodads followed. As we drew near my house, I felt a horrible dread in the pit of my stomach: Kelly's 1959 Ford Fairlane was nowhere to be seen, not in the driveway and not parked out front on the street.

Shit!

Chapter Fifteen

Big Brother

"**D**ammit!" I had to think fast. "Okay, Greg, here's the plan. Pull in my driveway. You and Paul make a dash for the front door, go in, lock the door and call the cops. I'll stay locked in the truck and let's hope for the best."

Greg came to a screeching stop in the driveway, but as he exited his door, Frankie intercepted him. The hodads had parked on the street and had bolted out of the muscle car before Frankie killed the engine. These guys were fast and got the jump on Greg and Paul. I heard Greg's body slam up against the side of the panel truck, followed by Frankie's squeaky voice.

"Okay, you faggoty surfer. Now you're going to find out what it feels like to have your ass kicked."

The rear door of the panel truck opened and Piggy stuck his head in. "Wanna step out, asshole," he said, "before I get in there and drag your sorry ass out." He held a bloodied handkerchief to his nose and looked infuriated. "You're gonna pay for my nose, fucker!"

I stepped out of the truck. Frankie had Greg pinned against the driver's door, his left forearm under Greg's chin and his right arm high in the air with his fist clenched, ready to strike. Greg's granny glasses had fallen onto the grass at his feet. Next to Frankie stood

Ratface, his arms locked on Paul's elbows, pinning them behind his back.

Piggy put his hand on my shoulder. "Don't even think of making a break for it. Your ass is mine." His body odor reeked like the smell of the pearl onions my mother steamed as a side dish for Sunday night supper—a dish I detested because of the awful body-odor-type smell and would not touch. Frankie seemed to enjoy taunting Greg with his right fist before he landed a blow.

In the second it takes to see your life flash before your eyes, the night became smothered in stillness. Crickets in the hedges stopped chirping; the sound of traffic on Venice Boulevard stopped; neighborhood dogs went silent. It was as if time itself had frozen, and with it, the rest of us.

Ratface was the first to notice something was wrong. He looked up toward the house, and jerked his head back in a panic, his eyes bulging as if he had seen the devil. "Ooooh, shit," I heard him mutter *sotto voce* as he let out his breath.

"Uh, Frankie." He whispered too softly for Frankie to break his concentration from taunting Greg. "*Frankie!*"

Frankie released his hold on Greg and turned toward Ratface. "What's wrong with you, Carmine?" he said. "Can't you see I'm busy?" Frankie took his cue from the horrified look on Carmine's face as he gestured toward the front of the house.

All six of us turned in unison. And there, standing under the archway on the top step of the porch, stood my brother Kelly, his rangy silhouette backlit from light spilling out of the open front door. Kelly stood in silence, the only indication that he was a living, breathing human being came from the glow of the Marlboro dangling from his mouth.

We stood there, unmoving, our eyes fixed to my brother's unreal wraith-like profile as if he were a demon ascended from hell. I would not have been surprised if he sprouted horns and his eyes glowed yellow in the night. I let out a long breath, felt a great sigh of relief and said a silent prayer. *Thank you, God. Thank you, God.*

Kelly knew what he was doing. He took his time finishing his cigarette and sized up the situation in the driveway. He allowed his ominous presence to sink in and let the hodads know the night was not going to end well for them. He flicked the Marlboro across the lawn, sparks pinwheeling in the night air until the butt landed at Frankie's boots. Time for business. He took his time descending the front porch steps and walked our way.

Ignoring the greasers, he stopped next to Greg. "What's going on here, Greg?" he said.

Greg picked up his glasses and cleaned them with his shirttail. "I have no idea, Kelly, These guys followed us here from A&W, and they obviously want to make trouble."

Frankie snickered. Kelly turned his six-foot-two frame to check him out. He towered over Frankie, who seemed to shrink as the seconds ticked by.

"Something funny, punk?" Kelly said. Frankie snickered again and would not look Kelly in the eyes, staring down at his boots instead. "Go ahead and laugh, asshole," Kelly said, "while you still have a set of teeth."

Then he turned toward Ratface. "God damn!" Kelly said with contempt in his voice. "You are *one* ugly fuck." Carmine averted his eyes and looked off toward the street.

Last in line, Kelly looked at Piggy. "You got something you want to say, Fat Boy?" he asked.

"I don't got nothin' to say," Piggy mumbled.

"Good," Kelly said. "You keep those chubby lips of yours shut, or I'll rearrange that nose of yours even further. And take your chubby paw off my brother's shoulder before I break it."

Piggy drew his hand back.

"You have to fight their battles?" Frankie asked.

Kelly took a few seconds to consider the question. "Not really, punk. I'm just here to level the playing field. How old are you guys, twenty? Twenty-one? You have to chase down sixteen year olds to prove how tough you are?"

Frankie nodded in Paul's direction. "That little shit flipped us off when they were leaving A&W," he said.

"Oh, *fuck you,* greaseball." Paul let it out. "These guys were trouble from the moment they entered A&W and parked next to us. First, they hassled some girlfriends of ours from school. Then when the girls shined them on, they decided to take their wrath out on us. C'mon, Kelly, let's kick their sorry asses."

Paul was a little scrapper and stood five feet seven. His older brother, Fran, taught him how to box at a young age. Paul had taken on one or two guys at the beach that were much bigger, and he used his quickness and agility to help him gain an advantage over his adversaries.

Kelly put his palm up in the air. "Put a lid on it, Paul. We're going to find out real soon how tough these shitbirds are." Kelly turned his attention to Frankie. "Frankie, huh? What kind of a name is that?"

Kelly looked down at Frankie's cuffed jeans and shiny black boots. "You some kind of fairy, *Frankie*? Are you a sissy boy who hangs out in Hollywood? Nobody cuffs their jeans like that anymore, *Frankie*, unless they're gay."

Kelly was pitching for a fight. Paul looked at me and gave a slight nod that I passed on to Greg—a signal that indicated should Frankie become unhinged and charge Kelly, we would be ready to jump in and start swinging.

"Okay, tough guy," Kelly said to Frankie. "Let's see how tough you *really* are. I'm going to let you throw the first punch. Go ahead, *cheese dick*. Give it your best shot."

Frankie looked like he was ready to explode, his face a distorted mask of hate and rage, and his fists clenched at his side. At first, I thought he was going to take Kelly up on his offer. Frankie glanced over his shoulder to see if Carmine and Piggy were going to back him up, but Ratface and Fat Boy had backed up into the street next to the open doors of the Skyliner. Frankie turned away from Kelly and retreated to his car where the threesome took their places with Frankie and Carmine in front, and Piggy in the back.

"You guys wait here," Kelly said to me and my buddies.

Kelly picked up a large rock by the driveway and walked up to the muscle car. Frankie started up the Skyliner and the night air filled once again with the roar of the glasspacks. Kelly leaned up close by Frankie's window. "If you take off before I finish here, I'll smash your windshield." The three hodads stared straight ahead as if they were in shock without looking at Kelly.

"Now listen up and listen up good," Kelly said. "If I ever catch you fuckin' assholes on this street again, I'll push your ugly fuckin' faces into the back of your heads. Now get the fuck out of here!"

Frankie drove straight ahead, and had to turn around at the dead end. He took it slow past Kelly, who was still in the street with the rock in his hand. When Frankie was halfway up Marvin Avenue, he stopped, revved his engine, and then let out the clutch, burning rubber all the way up to Venice Boulevard.

Kelly chuckled as he walked back to the lawn. "C'mon, let's go inside," he said. "I want to have a talk with you boys."

We sat at the dining room table. Kelly opened the icebox on the back porch and pulled out a six-pack of Coors. He handed us each a cold beer and asked how this whole incident came about.

Greg asked Kelly what was on all our minds. "Where is your car?"

"My fiancée met me when I got off work and followed me to my mechanic up on Pico Boulevard. I left my car for an oil change and tune-up tomorrow morning. She left a few minutes before you guys showed up with your friends."

We had a good laugh at that and chatted for a few minutes about Kelly's upcoming wedding in June.

Then Kelly took on a serious tone. "You know, that asshole Frankie made a good point when he asked if I had to fight your battles for you." He looked at me. "I'm getting married in a few months. I won't be around like I am now and you guys are going to have to learn to fight your own battles."

"I think we could have kicked their asses, Kelly," Paul said. "Of course, with a little help from you."

Kelly considered that and smiled. "You know what, Paul? I do believe you are right. Just you and me, we could have wiped their asses up and down Marvin while Walt and Greg sat on the porch and watched."

"Fuckin' A, tweedy!" Paul answered.

"So back to what I was saying," Kelly said. "It's a cruel world out there guys, and shit is going to happen to you whether you like it or not. You always have to be on your toes and be ready for whatever bad shit comes your way."

We finished our beers, and Paul and Greg stood up to leave. Paul had a midnight curfew and would have to deal with his dad, who would be waiting up for him. When they left, I walked up to Kelly who pulled his shirt off getting ready for bed.

"Thanks for tonight," I said. Then I threw my arms around his shoulders and gave him a hug. "You're the best brother a guy could ever ask for."

Chapter Sixteen

Norwegian Wood

I finished my story of the hodads around one o'clock in the morning. Catherine put the Beatles' *Rubber Soul* on her small stereo, placing the needle on the second song. As "Norwegian Wood" started, she reached out with her left hand. I stood up from the sofa, took her in my arms, and we slow danced to the opening chords of John's acoustic guitar, followed by George's sitar, and then John's nasal voice: "I once had a girl/or should I say, she once had me." I held Catherine close to my body as we swayed back and forth in a dream-like trance while listening to Lennon recount a late-night fling with a worldly woman of the night.

Halfway through the song, Catherine let go of my embrace and backed up a few steps. She looked up at me with her gorgeous blue-gray eyes, put her hands around my neck and beckoned me with her lips. In seconds, we kissed with abandon as our passion took over. Our tongues explored each other's mouths. My heart beat wildly as Catherine pulled me in harder and massaged the back of my neck, her fingernails pressing ever-so-softly into my flesh.

She broke our embrace to turn off the lamp. She blew out the candles, our time together noted by the wax that had spilled onto the holders. In the semi-dark, she took my hand and led me to her bedroom door. As we entered her room, I heard the final refrains of Lennon's voice: "So I lit the fire/Isn't it good, Norwegian Wood."

I awoke to the rhythmic thrum of rain pattering against the window next to Catherine's bed. A dingy, gray light crept across the walls of the bedroom.

I looked at the clock on the nightstand: 6:52 am. *Shit!* I never signed out for an overnight pass and would be considered AWOL if I didn't answer roll call at 8:30 a.m. back at Kishine. I never expected to be lying naked next to Catherine in the wee hours of Sunday morning, nope, never in a million years. She lay next to me, asleep, her dark hair a tangled mass splayed across the curve of her bare shoulders.

A large gust of wind followed by more rain shook the bungalow. I heard a clap of thunder in the distance. Catherine mumbled something unintelligible as she shifted her body and fell back into a deep sleep. She smelled of sweet German wine and lavender perfume.

I focused on a wall calendar and realized I would be turning twenty in a few days. My nineteenth year of life had been filled with many changes and surprises, none of them as pleasant as this. In the past nine months, I had gone through basic training at Ft. Bliss, Texas, moved on to Tigerland at Ft. Polk, Louisiana with an M.O.S (Military Occupational Specialty) of Light Weapons Infantry, which in turn, meant a plane ride to the jungles of Vietnam with no return ticket issued.

My first wound had not been a big deal. After getting proper stitches at base camp in Phan Thiêt, and a few days of R and R, I was sent back to the bush with my unit. The second wound, the ambush in Song Mao, was a game changer. I saw the enemy Chicom grenade land in front of me. I ran ahead of it in a V-shaped pattern to the grenade and angled my body. Shrapnel hit my left flank, the same side as the first wound. Several shards entered my left hip/buttock area and left leg.

My infantry training at Tigerland paid off. It helped that I had been wearing a PRC-25 (Prick-25) radio because it also absorbed several pieces of shrapnel, and to my amazement, still worked. It had spared my back from sustaining wounds.

I pushed my luck and stayed in bed a little longer, thinking about Catherine taking my hand after we slow danced and leading me into her bedroom. She sat me on her bed, lit a few candles, and undressed. She took her time, first removing her sweater and draping it over a chair. She unfastened her skirt and let it fall to the floor.

She had on a lacy black bra and black silk underwear. I felt my heart skip a notch and my temperature rise as I stared at her taut, athletic body. She had a slender, lithesome frame, the muscles in her legs and arms, sinuous and smooth. Her milky-white skin seemed to glow as the candles flickered shadows across the room. She removed her bra, and I admired her small, pert breasts. Her pink nipples, the color of rose petals, pointed outward with a slight stiffness.

She took my head in her hands and kissed me. Then she moved them to my clothes with an urgency she hadn't shown before, popping each button through its hole and pulling my shirt over my head. I helped speed up the process as her lips grazed across my face, neck, and shoulders. When she got down to my boxer underwear, I felt a tinge of pain in my left hip and sensed moisture coming through the cotton. I saw a small circle of blood leaching through my underwear in the area of my left hip. *Shit!*

Catherine started to remove my boxers, but I grabbed her hands. "Uh…, Catherine, I have a little problem."

She looked into my eyes with a confused look. She gave an understanding smile. "Oh, don't worry about it, Walt. It happens to the best of men."

What?! I thought. *What in the hell is she talking about?* Then it dawned on me. "Oh, my God!" I blurted out, breaking the gentle atmosphere. "Are you kidding me, L-T? I'm as hard as the god damn flagpole in front of Kishine Barracks. How could I not be—you are so gorgeous, so amazing. I have never been with such a beautiful woman in my life. The problem is, well, I seemed to have broken a stitch or two in my excitement to get out of my clothes."

Catherine let out a small laugh, unfazed by this news. "Well, guess what? You are in luck. I had four years of nurses' training before I went on for an advanced degree in physical therapy."

She walked to a small closet by the bathroom and returned with a leather satchel. She removed a stitching kit.

"Okay, off with your drawers so I can check this out. I'll get you patched up like new." I removed my boxer shorts and felt a little embarrassed. There was no doubt about my level of arousal. I snatched up my shorts and covered myself.

Catherine chuckled again. "It's not like I've never seen a hard-on, Walt. It's okay."

I decided it was better to look at the first-aid kit instead of her nipples, and watch her work on my leg. She removed a small bottle of alcohol, soaked a cotton ball, and dabbed at the blood around the broken suture. She removed the damaged stitch with a small pair of scissors. Next, she pulled out a long black nylon thread, inserted one end through a needle and tied it off.

Jesus! I thought. *This woman has been gulping down wine all night, and now she is going to perform minor surgery on my left hip. God help me!*

Catherine felt me tense and paused. "Don't worry, Walt. It will hurt a little, but you are a First Air Cav boonie rat. Piece of cake for you, right?"

I smiled and repeated her words. "Piece of cake, L-T."

After sewing me up anew, Catherine returned the satchel to the closet. She approached the bed and told me to lie on my back. She removed her panties and gently lay on top of me. She smothered my face with baby kisses and moved forward to put her breasts by my mouth. My heart pounded like crazy as I kissed her nipples. I felt overcome by a deep love for this beautiful woman. I was not a virgin. I had experienced a few sexual encounters with girls I knew from high school, but nothing compared to this.

Catherine sat up and straddled my body, settling her knees on each side of my hips in a way as to not rub against the fresh stitches. She reached between her legs and grasped my erect penis, and with one delicious push that sent me to a new state of delirium, slid me inside of her. We rocked back and forth for several minutes. She seemed as ready as I, and in a moment of intensity, we experienced orgasm at the same incredible moment. I had never imagined such pleasure could be possible—*heaven on earth*, I thought. I wanted the night to go on forever. After several more rounds, I cradled her in my arms, each of us in thrall from our lovemaking that continued as the candles burned low.

The drumming rain increased against the bungalow. As much as I wanted to stay and hold her again, I knew it was time to get back to Kishine Barracks before roll call. I also knew that if I stayed in bed with Catherine, the inevitable would happen—she would wake and her eyes would show a state of shock at seeing me naked in bed. She had way too much wine to drink and let her emotions take control, which led me into her bedroom instead on her couch, her original plan. It would be different if she hadn't been married; I would have stayed and said the hell with roll call.

I slid out of bed without waking her and put my clothes on. I noticed the stitches had held tight, and smiled as I replayed how she plied her nursing trade while being half in the bag. *Piece of cake,* I thought.

As I went to open her bedroom door, I heard the bed covers rustle as I walked to the bedroom door.

"Walt?"

We gazed at each other through sleepy eyes. I was relieved to be fully dressed, and her face did not register the shock I had anticipated.

"I had a wonderful time last night," she said. "So glad you came over for dinner. I even had fun learning that silly dance, the Surfer Stomp."

I stood in silence for a few moments, taking in her beautiful visage. I felt my throat grow tight. "Goodbye, Catherine."

I exited Catherine's home and into a light drizzle. The heavy rain had let up and the cool wind and droplets felt good against my face. I had no idea in which direction to head as I had been dropped off at Catherine's bungalow in total darkness the previous night. I came across an enlisted Army nurse cleaning up her front porch and asked for directions to Kishine Barracks. She told me the main highway to Kishine was about two hundred yards up the road and to make a left.

On the main highway, I looked east toward the city of Yokohama and the expansive width of Tokyo Bay with its pewter water reflecting the dull sky. Small whitecaps formed on the bay from the brisk wind. Huge clouds the color of slate, their bellies laden with rain were heading my way. I knew in a matter of minutes I would be drenched.

Then something miraculous happened: a bold ray of sunshine managed to penetrate a break in the clouds and a long rainbow appeared, stretching from the port of Yokohama across Tokyo Bay to the eastern edges of the Boso Peninsula. I had never seen a rainbow that massive. I stood there, transfixed by the beautiful luminous hues of the prism arching in a giant bow over the bay.

I remembered studying Genesis in second grade religion class at Holy Spirit, and Sister Scholastica talking about Noah and the great flood. When the rain stopped and the waters subsided, a giant rainbow greeted Noah as his ark came to rest upon the land. Sister Scholastica explained to us that a rainbow came to symbolize peace and hope. Then God said to Noah: "This is the sign that I'm giving for all ages to come, of the covenant between me and you and every living creature with you…"

Maybe God was making a covenant between Himself and me. Maybe, just maybe, if I continued to pray and helped Lt. Coleman with his patients, I would never see the face of war again; maybe I would live another day, another month, or another year, and return to The World to be reunited with my family.

Then, as suddenly as the rainbow appeared, it vanished. Mushroom-shaped clouds billowed across the bay. A streak of lightning lit up the Boso Peninsula, and I heard thunder rumble in the distant sky. I turned, put the hood up on my windbreaker, and headed back up the hill to Kishine.

Photo with siblings. Bottom left to right, Kathleen, Maureen, Neal (center), Me (in shorts), Kelly, Virginia (top) circa 1952

Senior high school photo. Senior Photo, St. John Vianney High School, Los Angeles, Ca. June '65"

Head shot with US on my lapels."Basic Training, Ft. Bliss, Tx Aug. '66"

Photo of me wearing a steel pot and holding my M-16 rifle (first week in Phan Thiêt)

Photo taken for mom and family taken in downtown Phan Thiet is Feb. '67

Standing in group photo (Arrow pointing to my head). Second Platoon, Charlie Comp., 2nd Battalion, 7th Infantry, 1st Cavalry Division (Airmobile)

Soldiers sitting against fence. April '67…getting ready to deploy to Song Mao. Randy Kent (center) Randy Caswell (Kneeling)

Me, lying in bed with Purple Heart case opened. April '67, 8th Field Hospital, Nha Trang,...Award of the Purple Heart by Gen. William Westmoreland"

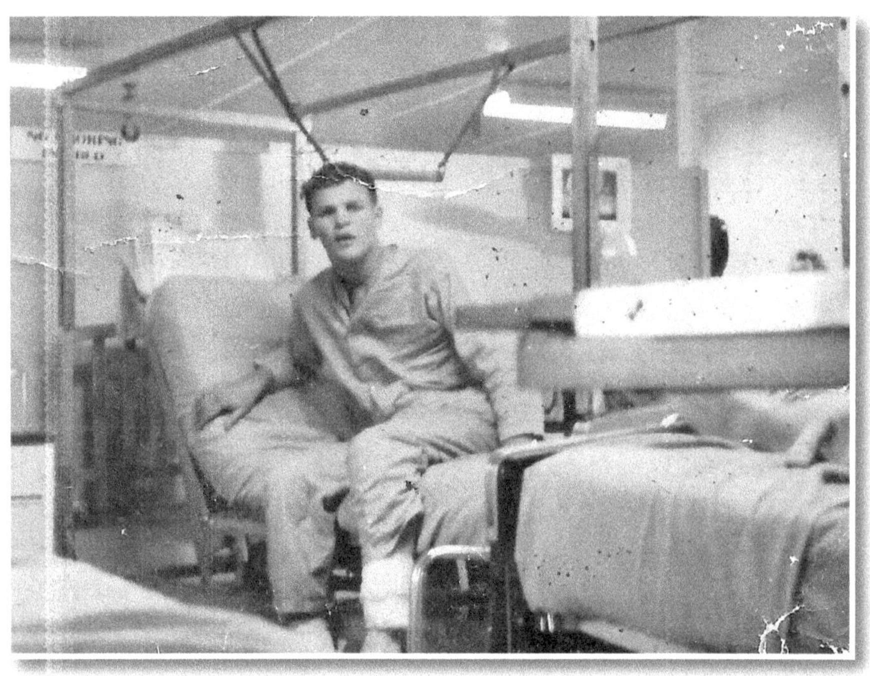

String up in bed. Me, 'on the mend' at 8th Field Hospital, Nha Trang, April '67

Sgt. Porter

Chapter Seventeen

Little Buddha

"Scuze, please. Scuze, please."

I had been lost in thought, easy to do with Catherine on my mind. I looked up from my bench and saw one of the Japanese groundsmen waving a small brown bag in my direction. He stood by the pond.

"Feed fish? Feed fish?" he said.

He gave the bag a few more shakes and I understood it was feeding time for the koi fish that inhabited the pond.

"Sure," I said. "Why not?"

I had nothing else to do and thought it would be fun. I approached him and took the bag. His fellow groundsman had tossed small clumps of bread into the pond. I followed suit and soon all three of us were tossing bread into the water.

At first, nothing much happened. A few koi fish swam by and nibbled on the crumbs. In a flash of kaleidoscopic color, the pond turned into a swirling, roiling mass of red, blue, yellow, orange, gold, and tan. Koi fish emerged from the depths and fought each other for every floating morsel. They scooped and dove back down as they jockeyed for space and an easy meal. I had never seen anything like it. I had no idea there were so many koi fish in the pond. The colors were amazing, vibrant, and reminded me of the rainbow I had seen when I left Catherine's bungalow a few weeks back.

Both groundsmen were laughing and seemed to be having the time of their lives as they continued to taunt the fish with larger clumps of bread. Later, I discovered the meaning of koi fish in Japan was good fortune or luck. They are also associated with perseverance through adversity, strength, or purpose. These colorful, ornamental versions of the common carp date back to early Nineteenth Century Japan.

Feeding the fish with the groundsmen instilled a feeling, a special bond with these two kindred souls. I also felt gratitude that they took the time to invite me to partake in their afternoon ritual. I felt as if another small miracle had unfolded that special day.

Over twenty years ago, my country dropped two atomic bombs on the Japanese cities of Hiroshima and Nagasaki, both located approximately four hundred miles southwest of Yokohama. The blasts killed between 129,000 and 226,000 people, and many more would die from radiation poisoning. Yet these two gentle souls harbored no animosity toward me, an American. I sensed they understood everything about me being a wounded soldier in recovery, and the miracle and ineffable joy flowing through my veins because I would be going back to The World that very evening. I, too, began to understand the warmth in their hearts as we continued to throw bread upon the water.

We eventually ran out of provisions and, once again, the pond became still. I bowed to the groundsmen, brought my palms together in prayer, and said, "Thank you. Thank you." They smiled and both bowed back in my direction as was their custom. Afterward, they went back to their business of tending to the tea garden.

. . .

As the afternoon wore on, I decided to stop ignoring my hunger pangs and went for lunch. Entering the enlisted men's mess hall, I heard Specialist Green call out.

"Hey, Madigan. Over here. Get your chow and join us."

Green sat at a table in the back with two other soldiers from our reassignment ward. I filled my tray with soup, salad, and sandwich, grabbed a lemonade, and joined Green and his buddies.

"Madigan," Green said. "This is Private First Class Meadows and Specialist Henry Kavanaugh, another Screaming Eagle. They are in our ward but haven't received reassignment orders yet. I told them all about your morning with Sgt. Brooks, and we have been laughing ever since."

I didn't know Meadows or Kavanaugh personally, but I recognized them from the barracks. Like me, Meadows was First Cav; he also had similar shrapnel wounds in his lower extremities. Hopefully, he would be soon going back to the states.

Green continued. "I was telling Kavanaugh and Meadows about you surfing at the beach in Phan Thiêt and getting buzzed by that squad of Hueys. Do you want to add anything?"

"Sure," I said. "That day was so unreal, man. The waves at Little Buddha were perfect, and I had a blast putting on a show for all the boonie rats in Second Platoon. And then mail call later that day—even more unreal. Allow me to explain." I launched into my story in between bites of food.

After a month in-country, my company was returning to our base camp, LZ Betty, from a ten-day Search and Destroy mission. As we flew in low over the South China Sea, the Huey pilots decided to buzz the nearby sampans, junks, and smaller vessels to intimidate any enemy soldiers who might have been lurking aboard, storing rice and weapons among other things. Only I was paying attention to the incoming waves at Little Buddha—a beach adjacent to our airstrip.

Randy Kent, who I knew from Tigerland, looked at me. "Man, conditions are perfect today, Madigan."

Kent was an excellent surfer from San Pedro, California, and like me, began surfing in his early teens. He added, "You have an east swell with an offshore wind coming from the west northwest. Little Buddha is a beach break and waves peak high in the middle so you can take off either left or right. The surf is fairly consistent there with a deep ground swell, and I'm noticing perfect combers coming in at three and four feet."

I was impressed with Kent's knowledge of the local beaches. "Right now," he said, "we are at the tail end of the Southeast Asian typhoon season. Typhoons from the Philippines bring storms along the South Vietnam coast and that makes the waves larger than normal."

"Jesus, Kent," I said. "How do you know all this stuff?"

"I went to the library in San Pedro before leaving for Vietnam. I wanted to be well-versed on surfing conditions before landing in-country. You never know when you might get an opportunity to surf." He said he had surfed Little Buddha a few times since we had arrived in South Vietnam in early February. "But I've never seen conditions this good. Remember that little Chinese guy who always wears that pith helmet when he comes by and collects our empty C ration cans? We call him Chang. I'm not certain that is his real name. Anyway, he has a small business renting surfboards on the beach near Little Buddha. Some of them are in decent shape."

Perfect, I thought.

Five minutes later, the grunts in my company were jumping off the Huey Slicks at LZ Betty airstrip. Most of the men headed to the mess hall for a real meal after having eaten C rations for the last ten days. Some headed for the makeshift showers on base to wash off the accumulated filth from the jungle, which we had patrolled with rigor for the last ten days.

I hustled over to my hooch, unloaded my ruck and M14 rifle, grabbed a smaller pack and loaded it with my .45 caliber pistol, a KA-BAR knife, some additional ammo, a towel, and a pair of swimming trunks. Shouldering my gear, I headed down the switchback road that led to Little Buddha Beach.

Sure enough, I ran into Chang at his crude surfboard rental stand crafted of thrown together materials. He seemed happy to see me. He started shaking both my hands and bowed as was his custom. He repeated, "Xin Chao," several times, the Vietnamese way of showing respect and saying hello. He gestured at his collection of surfboards and said, "You surf today, GI? My boards very good, number one. I give very good deal for two hour."

One board, a Dewey Weber, caught my attention. It was similar to my own Con surfboard, which was nine feet three inches long. The Dewey Weber was a little under nine feet. It was in good condition and already had several layers of paraffin wax applied.

"This is the one," I said. I handed Chang three American dollar bills.

Chang was a happy guy and thanked me profusely. "Xin cam on. Xin cam on," he exclaimed. "You number one GI!"

Chang's teeth were a reddish color and almost worn down to the nub from chewing betel nut. This psychoactive stimulant popular among the Vietnamese was made from betel leaf, areca nut, and slaked lime juice. One time when Chang was collecting empty C ration cans in our commons area, he offered some betel nut to Caswell, who gave it a try. He said it tasted bitter and spicy; then he spit it out. He experienced a mild high and said it was like drinking six cups of coffee.

As usual, Chang had a wad of betel nut in his cheek and more in his pocket. He offered me some. I laughed. "No thanks," I said. "Gotta hit the waves."

I grabbed my board and headed to the breakwater. Kent was right. Beautiful peaks cropped up and broke in sections. I knew from surfing beach breaks in California that my patience would be rewarded if I waited to get a feel for the rhythm of the sets, which usually came in patterns of three or four waves. I hoped my muscle memory would kick in as I paddled out to the farthest set.

Unlike California, where the water temperature in my area ranged from 55 to 60 degrees Fahrenheit on any given day, the water in the South China Sea was at least 75 degrees. Though I hadn't surfed in six months, I had one advantage—I was at least fifteen pounds lighter than the day I entered the Army. I also felt strong. Lugging around a seventy-pound ruck all day in the steamy, hot jungle, along with various pouches of ammo and bandoleers of 7.62 millimeter bullets for the M60 machine guns, got me into shape real fast. If the sets came in four waves, I learned to wait for the last swell in the lineup in case I wiped out and would not get pounded trying to get back outside the break.

My first attempts at catching waves ended in disaster as the nose of the surfboard pearled while I attempted my takeoff. I ended up wiping out and going over the falls.

I had to make an adjustment for riding a shorter board than I was used to. I backed up six inches or so to the rear of the board and that did the trick. My footing started to feel more natural and my muscle memory kicked in. I caught my first ride of the day, a perfectly formed three-foot comber that had my name on it as the luminous, blue-green swell headed in my direction. I turned my surfboard toward shore, began paddling at full speed, and soon felt the forward motion of the swell pick up the back of my board. As I gained speed, I jumped to my feet, rotated the board to the right with equal weight on my front and back feet and started gliding down the face of the swell, heading down the line as the wave crested and broke to my rear.

The ride was pure bliss as I drove down the face and felt the spray exploding at my heels. As the wave began to close out, I leaned back and pushed down with my right foot, I steered the board with my left foot up the face of the wave, performing a perfect kick out. I went over the lip before the wave exploded into white soupy foam.

I could not believe I was surfing in the South China Sea as a deadly war played out a few klicks away from the beach at Little Buddha. It was a far cry from my home base at Sunset Beach in Pacific Palisades.

After I found my sweet spot for taking off on the Dewey Weber, I began to catch larger waves. After one particularly good ride in which I was able to tuck, grab a rail and shoot through a barrel to the other side before the wave closed out, I heard whistling, catcalls, and hollers coming from the cliffs above the beach. Looking up, I saw soldiers from my platoon sitting back, drinking beer, smoking cigarettes and having a good time. I waved to them and got more whistles and catcalls.

I was exhausted near the end of the afternoon and ready to quit when I turned and saw a perfectly formed five-foot, blue-green swell heading my way. The wave was about thirty yards out. I turned the nose of my board toward shore, looked up at the grunts watching me, and said to myself, *"Okay, boonie rats. It's showtime!"*

My timing was perfect as the swell picked up my board. I jumped up, turned right, and fired down the line. Just before taking off on the wave, I heard a tremendous roar behind me, and figured it was two F-4 Phantom jets flying in low as they made their way to Cam Ranh Bay north of Phan Thiêt. At that moment, it occurred to me that I had not hung five that day, and decided this was the perfect wave for such a stunt. After all, my fellow grunts wanted a show.

Speeding down the face of the swell, I positioned my board so it was midline of the wave face. Then I began a cross-step shuffle toward the nose of the board keeping my balance in the center. As I approached the nose to hang five toes over, I again heard an ear-piercing roar over my head followed by a blast of wind that almost knocked me over the falls.

I looked up. I was being buzzed by a squad of six Huey gunships. The door gunner on the chopper above me swiveled his M60 machine gun so he could lean out and flash me the ubiquitous peace sign. His shit-eating grin told me what he thought of my stunt. It was easily the most surreal experience of my life.

Still riding the wave, in some kind of miracle, I managed to hang five toes over the nose. As the wave closed out in front of me, I had no time to back up for a kick out, so I finished the show by jumping off the nose and doing a cannonball into the roiling white foam.

Mail Call

By 12:30 p.m. the wind picked up and the surf started to get blown out, my cue to pack it in. I got back to my hooch around one. Tired and happy, with my last bit of strength, I peeled off my trunks in favor of a clean T-shirt and a pair of Army-issue boxers in preparation for a much-deserved three-hour nap in my sleeping roll.

Before crashing, I asked Caswell to be sure and wake me in time for Class Six provisions followed by mail call. My hooch smelled of wet canvas, bug juice, diesel fuel, and gun oil. My improvised living space consisted of two US Army half tents fastened together tautly and covered with several poncho liners to keep out moisture from the persistent monsoon rainstorms. I also surrounded it with sandbags to keep it from blowing away when Chinook transport choppers flew overhead and landed nearby at LZ Betty.

Every item in my hooch was covered with a thin layer of red dust as a result of the constant air traffic. When we got back to base camp after humping in the bush, I protected my M14 rifle by wrapping it in a towel. Sgt. Porter often stressed how important it was to have that weapon clean, well-oiled, and ready to lock and load at a moment's notice.

I felt as if I had been asleep for only fifteen minutes when Caswell shook my shoulders.

"Get your ass up, Madigan!" he screamed in my ears. "You don't want to miss your goodies at the EM Club."

At sixteen hundred hours, the Enlisted Men's club would dole out my two beers, two Cokes, and two packs of Chesterfields. Located next to command quarters at LZ Betty, the EM Club was a large tent, forty by fifty feet, and surrounded with emptied ammunition boxes we filled with sand and rocks stacked eight feet high for protection against an enemy mortar attack. The floor consisted of wooden pallets covered and nailed down with half inch sheets of plywood. Inside was a makeshift bar on long Formica folding tables where soldiers could purchase beer, wine, and whiskey. Smaller tables and folding chairs gave us a place to relax with our drinks.

Besides beer, sodas and cigarettes, Class Six provisions also consisted of stationery, envelopes, and writing utensils so the soldiers of Charlie Company could write home. We didn't need stamps; we could write "free" in the upper right hand corner of the envelope.

Some of the men in Charlie Company didn't drink alcohol, and I was happy to trade a can of Coke or two for two beers.

After receiving my Class Six booty, I pulled up a chair in the EM Club and sat with our Second Platoon squad leader, Roger Powers, and fellow grunts, Randy Kent and Randy Caswell. Other soldiers from our platoon sat at nearby tables. I popped open a Schlitz, lit a Chesterfield, and observed the men relaxing in the club.

Most of the soldiers in Charlie Company were my age, nineteen, or a few years older. I remembered Sgt. Porter telling me that the average age of a US soldier in World War II was 26, in Korea, 24. Times had changed. These men were not fighting in Vietnam by choice. They were draftees because they didn't have the wherewithal to attend college or come from wealthy families that had the means to get a doctor's note declaring them unfit for military service.

My loophole was a college student deferment when I started Community College in February of 1966. I was eighteen then and more interested in majoring in surfing, drinking beer, and chasing girls. I was failing Merchandising, a boring class, and decided to withdraw instead of getting a failure notice. That set off a red flag with the college administrators who alerted the Draft Board of my decision. Since I was not carrying a full load of fifteen units, a few weeks later I received my Notice to Appear for Induction in downtown Los Angeles. My deferment had evaporated into thin air. Instead of teenaged antics, I now had the camaraderie of my fellow grunts in the EM Club tent.

I heard the distinct laugh of Sgt. Roach, our machine gunner, as he held court at another table with other Black soldiers of Second Platoon. Most of the Black grunts in Charlie Company kept to themselves at the EM club. Little by little, I was gaining their respect as we engaged in more severe firefights with the enemy on Search and Destroy missions. In time, they trusted me to cover their backs as I held my own.

I caught the eye of the Roachman, raised my beer as a salute. Sgt. Roach smiled and nodded back. Over half of the men in Charlie Company were African American because Blacks were drafted at a disproportionately higher rate than Whites. Vietnam was the first major US war in which Black and White soldiers were fully integrated.

"I heard you got buzzed by six Huey gunships while hanging five at Little Buddha," Kent said.

"Oh, my God, Kent," I said. "It was fucking unreal! More like surreal. I could have reached up and touched the skids of the chopper above my head. The back draft from the blades almost blew me off my board, and the door gunner flashed me the peace sign with a huge grin on his face. And the waves, man. They were perfect groomers coming in at three and four feet. I was the only grunt surfing today. It felt like having Malibu all to myself."

. . .

At 1630 hours a small military flatbed truck loaded with mailbags and packages pulled up in front of the EM Club. Soldiers gathered around the truck as the two mail specialists unloaded bags and packages designated for each platoon in Charlie Company. Any soldier back from the bush cherished this moment above all others. A letter from home was a treasured gift. It was the only link a soldier had to his life back in The World, allowing him to temporarily escape the horrors of war.

Men gathered in front of the EM Club waiting to hear their name called out for a letter or package. I attended mail call with mixed feelings: I was thankful to get a handful of letters from family and friends from home, but felt badly for the guys who did not receive either a letter or package. It broke my heart to see these soldiers leave empty-handed; sometimes I even felt guilty.

Specialist Fourth Class Keating, our mail specialist, jumped down from his flatbed truck, grabbed two mail sacks for Second Platoon, and said, "Who in the hell is this Private First Class Madigan?"

I smiled and raised my can of Schlitz. "That would be me, Specialist."

Keating narrowed his eyes with suspicion. "What the fuck!" he said. "Do you have some kind of fan club?"

I had no idea what he was talking about. "The only fan club I have are my fellow boonie rats in Charlie Company. They know I always have their backs when the shit hits the fan."

That got a few laughs and whistles from some of the soldiers. Keating reached in the first mailbag and pulled out a three-inch stack of mail fastened with several rubber bands and tossed it to me. "Those are all for you. Plus," he said, "you have over twenty packages on the other flatbed."

At first I thought he was joking. But when I unfastened the rubber bands, I realized Keating wasn't joking. Six months later when I was back in The World, my sister Maureen confessed to me that when anyone called the house, my mother would not "request" that the other person on the line send her son a letter or package, she would "demand" they send a letter, if not a goody package.

My tough-as-nails mother, Nellie, having raised eight children, was very protective of her brood. She was popular with the nuns at my parochial school, Holy Spirit, and as head of the Mother's Club, she wielded a lot of power over the women in that organization. Hence, the surplus of mail and packages that day in Vietnam.

When mail call ended, Kent, Caswell, and Powers helped me with the packages, and we set them on a table. The atmosphere in the EM Club changed to stony silence as soldiers read letters from home, smoked cigarettes, and drank their sodas and beer.

Some of the grunts in Charlie Company received Dear John letters from girlfriends back home; worse yet, some from wives. I could always tell which soldiers received the dreadful news by their hollowed-out eyes and stunned expressions.

I read one or two of my own letters. I paused and took a long look around the club. I caught the eyes of soldiers who hadn't received a letter or package from home, and when our eyes met, I noticed they looked down at their boots, as if feeling shame for not receiving any word or parcel from home. *Aw shit,* I thought, *this ain't fucking right.*

What I did next was an act that has stayed with me, even some fifty-plus years later. Maybe it was God whispering in my ear, or perhaps my mother. It didn't matter; I knew what I had to do. I stood up, grabbed a package, and yelled to the first soldier who had not received mail.

"Hey, Peterson," I shouted. "Heads up!" I tossed the package his way. "Hey, 'Spina! Look alive, man. I tossed him the next package.

"You, Westbrook! Coming your way." On and on, I continued until there was only one package left that I kept for myself.

"Okay, boonie rats," I yelled to all. "I'm going to count to three, and on three, I want you to open your package, take out a treat, be it cookies or brownies or candy or whatever, and then pass that package to the grunt next to you.

Then I shouted at the top of my voice: "LET'S HAVE A GOD DAMN PARTY!" And just like that, the funereal atmosphere in the room dissolved.

Sgt. Roach popped an 8-track into his player and music from The Left Banke filled the air: "*Just walk away, Renée, You won't see me follow you back home…*"

The atmosphere turned festive in the wake of this small miracle. Every soldier in that room shared something with another soldier. We joked, laughed, and even shared our beers. The Roachman amplified the music to match the uplifted vibe of the party.

One package contained white jockey underwear. Sandoval, Pruitt, and McClure donned them over their heads so their ears poked out of the leg holes and performed a grunt rendition of the Can Can while the Left Banke continued their ballad. "…from deep inside the tears that I'm forced to cry…"

My stack of mail filled my grasp. Knowing I couldn't possibly read every letter, I decided to distribute a few to my fellow grunts.

"Here you go, Bailey," I said. "It's a letter from my blonde cousin, Mary. I know you have a crush on her. See what she has to say, man."

I walked up to Private First Class Dawson, one of Sgt. Roach's ammo bearers, and handed him a letter from my Aunt Dena, who was married to the president of a brewery in Omaha; she usually put a few bucks in with her note. Dawson was a quiet Black man who stood in the shadow of Sgt. Roach. He seemed surprised when I approached him. He looked up at me with his widened eyes, his pupils dilated and black as the jungle night.

"Here you go, Dawson. A letter from my rich aunt back in the states. Tell me what she has to say. And don't be holding out on me, man, in case there are a few buckeroos in that envelope." I laughed.

I felt a hand on my shoulder and turned to see Sgt. Roach towering over me. He had a huge smile on his face as he handed me a joint the size of a small cigar.

"Take a hit of this," he said, "and you won't be feeling any pain, my friend."

I took a hit and coughed uncontrollably. "God damn, Sergeant. That's some strong shit."

"You better believe it, Surfer Joe," he said. "The local gooks call it Black Mo, and by the way, you can call me Roachman from here on out. And, man, that was quite a show you put on today at Little Buddha. My boys and me were sitting on the cliff smoking Black Mo, drinking beer, and watching you catch one wave after another. Where did you learn to surf like that?"

"I'm from Southern California and I started surfing when I was fifteen—anywhere from the Ventura County Line north down to Malibu, Sunset, Redondo Breakwater, Doheny, Trestles, and south to San Diego."

We both focused on PFC Dawson who held the letter from my aunt. He had opened the letter, but it didn't look like he was reading. He seemed disinterested in the letter itself. Instead, he held it to his nose and sniffed it along with the envelope.

Roachman turned to me. "You know, Madigan, Dawson don't read. He probably thinks that letter came from his grandma back home. She raised him after both his parents died from drug overdoses. But that's okay. I look after him and set him straight in Charlie

Company. He's a damn good ammo bearer and always with me when the shit hits the fan."

"Aw, shit, Roachman. I had no idea he didn't read. I feel like an asshole handing him that letter."

"No, no, no," he said, waving his hand to dismiss the thought. "Are you kidding, man? What you did was good. Just look at the smile on his face as he stares at that envelope and thinks his grandma sent him a note from home. And sharing all those packages with the grunts from Second Platoon? That was mind-blowing, to say the least. You some kind of hero now, Surfer Joe, and don't you forget it."

. . .

Later that evening I was assigned night guard duty along with Randy Kent and Willie Moore. The base camp at LZ Betty was surrounded with thick circular coils of concertina wire. Bulldozers cleared a two-hundred-yard area in front of the strands, dubbed the "kill zone." It was laced with booby traps, trip flares, and claymore mines.

Bunkers were positioned twenty yards apart on the perimeter, mostly large 6 x 6 holes fortified with timber, sandbags, and large rocks. Every other bunker had a M60 machine gun mounted on a tripod in case the enemy had any thoughts of pulling a sneak attack. Base camp security required twenty-four-hour perimeter guard duty.

Our bunker was located on the easternmost section of LZ Betty, north of the air strip. Beyond the kill zone were bluffs with Little Buddha Beach at the base. I could hear waves lapping on the shore below and thought about my surfing adventure earlier that day. I set up two claymore mines at the base of the concertina wire and attached two small bells to the strands above them in case a sapper was bold enough to climb the cliffs to try and slip through the wire and attack our position.

Kent and Moore laid out several ammo clips for their M16 rifles, and I did the same for my M79 grenade launcher and M14 rifle. We took shifts of two hours each. This allowed us to have a four-hour rest until our shift repeated. I took the first watch at 2100 hours. Randy and Willie climbed into their sleeping rolls and fell asleep.

Soon our position was shrouded in darkness. It was a cloudless night, which was rare, and moonless. Above me a canopy of brilliant twinkling stars arched across the night sky and descended in an easterly direction into the inky black South China Sea. An inlet located two hundred meters north of Little Buddha beach formed a natural harbor. Junks, sampans, and other Vietnamese fishing vessels were moored there, each tied together.

The smell of cooked fish and rice wafted in the air, and I could hear the soft chatter of Vietnamese as the fishermen ate their dinner. Most of these men lived on their vessels and rarely set foot on dry land. Attached to the stern of each vessel was a colored light, and if I blurred my eyes just so, the lights appeared as a multi-colored jeweled bracelet floating in the air as the boats bobbed and weaved with the incoming tide.

I decided to have a cigarette and crawled back to where Moore and Kent were sleeping. I put my poncho over my head and cupped my hands together when I flicked my lighter so I would not give away our position. When I turned, I was startled to see Sgt. Porter standing at the base of the bunker. I never heard his approach.

He looked at me and smiled. "Mind if I share that Chesterfield with you, Madigan."

"Jesus, Sergeant, you scared the shit out of me. You appeared out of nowhere like a ghost."

"You're lucky I wasn't an enemy sapper. Otherwise, I easily could have thrown a satchel loaded with explosives into your bunker, and you three soldiers would be history. Having a smoke is okay on guard duty, but never, ever, turn your back to your forward observation area. You can throw a poncho over your head and quickly light your ciggie with cupped hands, but always be looking forward. The VC are very crafty and know where each guard bunker is located on the perimeter of this base."

Then he said a line I would hear in a film several years later: "Keep your friends close, Madigan, but keep your enemy closer."

At six feet one inch, Sgt. Jeffery Porter was a well-built rugged soldier in his mid-twenties. He was handsome, and bore a vague resemblance to the actor Tab Hunter. Porter was born to be an infantry soldier with good instincts when it came to figuring out Charlie's next move.

One night, while out in the bush on a Search and Destroy mission, he convinced the commanding officer of Charlie Company to change our position—at 0100 hours. We had been tailed all day by a VC sniper and his intuition told him that our position was on the enemy's radar.

It felt strange to saddle up and move two kilometers to the northwest in total darkness, but never-the-less, we moved out. At 0200 hours, we heard the distinct popping sound of enemy mortars being fired followed by the explosions. *Karrumph…karrumph…karrumph.* The VC were dropping shells in the position we moved out of only an hour before.

Our shared cigarette grew hot and after taking another drag, Porter stubbed out the Chesterfield in the dirt. I was glad we were in the quiet and not out on a Search and Destroy mission. It was then we heard what sounded like the rumble of artillery at the base of a mountain located three klicks southwest of LZ Betty. Each boom was followed by a bright light as if someone was walking through the jungle taking pictures with a giant flashbulb. Sgt. Porter pulled his field binoculars and studied the attack with quiet intensity.

"What's going on, Sergeant?" I asked.

"Looks like Bravo Company is getting hit with an enemy mortar attack," Porter said. Our PRC-25 radio crackled at a low volume, and we could hear a lieutenant from Bravo Company giving coordinates and requesting an artillery barrage.

"Fuckin' slopes are stepping up their game and getting closer and closer to our base camp as the days roll on," Porter said. "I won't be surprised if they attack LZ Betty any day now. But that's okay; we'll be ready for those motherfuckers once they approach the kill zone. When they get there, we will light up the night with parachute flares and shoot them like fish in a barrel."

Next we heard the chatter of small arms fire in the distance. Ribbons of enemy green tracer fire illuminated the night sky, followed by streams of red tracer fire from Bravo Company. It had the appearance of a bizarre light show as the incandescent glow of the red and green tracers criss-crossed in an X pattern across the pitch black sky.

"Rest up tonight, Madigan," Porter said. "Charlie Company is moving out tomorrow at 0900 hours along with Delta Company to a province about sixty kilometers northeast of Phan Thiêt."

He picked up his radio and rifle in preparation to check out other positions on the perimeter. Before he left, he said, "I heard about mail call today."

I didn't know how to reply. Maybe Sgt. Porter thought I was showboating or trying to direct attention to myself and didn't approve of my actions.

"They're a bunch of great guys." It was the only thing I could think to say.

"You did well, soldier," he said. "Keep it up."

"Thanks, Sergeant."

Song Mao

I grabbed a cup of coffee after lunch in the mess hall and rejoined Green, Meadows, and Kavanaugh at their table. I would probably never see any of these soldiers again after boarding the C-141 Starlifter tonight on my journey home. It was fun trading stories with them about our different lives, but we all had one thing in common: we had survived fierce combat with the enemy and gotten off easy with non-life threatening wounds.

"So, Madigan, how did you get wounded the second time and end up here at Kishine?" Specialist Kavanaugh asked. "Green told us you walked right into an NVA ambush. Care to share the story with us? If not, that's cool. I will understand."

"No, that's fine," I said. "Man, oh man, it was one hell of a day, and I had no clue it would be my last day in combat." I proceeded to tell my story.

In early April 1967, Charlie and Delta companies of the Second Battalion, 7th Cavalry, 1st Cavalry Division (Airmobile) were deployed from LZ Betty to Song Mao, a town fifty-six kilometers northeast of Phan Thiêt, located in a province called Bình Thuận.

Song Mao Base Camp was equipped with a long airstrip, and we arrived in two Air Force C-130 Hercules aircraft. The Hercules was the prime transport for airdropping troops, oversized cargo, and equipment into hostile areas. In an aerial delivery role, the C-130 Hercules could airdrop loads up to 42,000 pounds, or use its high flotation landing gear to land and deliver cargo on rough, dirty strips. The airstrip was also capable of landing the two workhorse jets of the Vietnam war: the Douglas A-4 Skyhawk and the McDonnell Douglas F-4 Phantom II.

Song Mao Base Camp was mainly populated by South Vietnamese soldiers known as the Army of the Republic of Vietnam (ARVN.) A US Special Forces unit had been deployed to Song Mao two weeks earlier. Charlie and Delta companies were there as backup as well as the Green Berets for the ARVN forces. Army intelligence had knowledge of a large contingent, possibly a battalion of enemy North Vietnamese Army (NVA) moving into the surrounding area. ARVN and NVA soldiers had recently been engaged in fierce combat.

Sgt. Porter informed each man in Second Platoon that we needed to stay focused and alert as we would be severely tested in the next few weeks. He reminded us that we would be facing an aggressive, battle-savvy enemy.

Most of the firefights Charlie Company had encountered up to this point were against Viet Cong soldiers, South Vietnamese insurgent guerrilla fighters sympathetic to the communist cause. Soon we would encounter combat trained soldiers of the North Vietnamese Army, who were well-equipped with mortars and Russian made AK-47 rifles.

On April 4th, we were alerted to saddle up. Charlie Company was being called out on a one-day operation known as a Mini-Cav. We would not be carrying full rucks.

Our commanding officer had received distress calls from an ARVN lieutenant and his RTO, that is, his radio telephone operator.

Apparently, the ARVN platoon had become separated from the main company and walked into an enemy ambush. The lieutenant and his RTO were the only survivors. Charlie Company's objective was to locate the two South Vietnamese soldiers, and gather intelligence on the ambush location.

Because we were not carrying full rucks, I doubled up on ammo pouches, two extra canteens of water, and extra fragmentation grenades by attaching them all to my web gear. As an afterthought, I attached two smoke grenades.

I was informed that I would be assigned RTO for Second Platoon. Our regular RTO, Specialist Boswell, came down with a nasty case of malaria and was sent to recover at the Third Field Hospital at Tan Son Nhut Air Base near Saigon. I was friends with Boswell and was familiar with operating the transmission radio. The bad news: I would have to hump the cumbersome PRC-25 radio, affectionately known as the Prick-25. It weighed over thirty pounds and was a real ass-kicker. The good news: I would be assigned to walk with our platoon's executive officer, Lieutenant Anderson, and would not be walking point. Our position was usually in the center of the diamond-shaped formation.

Charlie Company loaded up on Bell UH-1D transport helicopters, also known as Hueys though commonly referred to as Slicks, and flew to a destination eight klicks southwest of Song Mao Base Camp. Fortunately, the ARVN lieutenant had a red smoke grenade attached to his web gear. He was instructed to set it off when he saw the Air Cav choppers approach his position. It was nothing short of a miracle finding the two ARVN soldiers before the VC had a chance to hunt them down and execute them.

We saw his smoke and descended into light forest, terrain consisting of various types of scrub, deep ravines, razor-sharp elephant grass, and an occasional copse of bamboo and teak trees. I saw sunbaked anthills scattered about, some as tall as a man. This was high country, and we were relieved to find out we would not be slogging through swamps or rice paddies.

As RTO with Commanding Officer Lt. Anderson, I was present when Captain Hudson, the CO of Charlie Company, and Sgt. Porter approached the ARVN soldiers with our Kit Carson scout. These scouts were daring young Vietnamese men recruited by the Army to act as interpreters and guides. Some were former Viet Cong combatants and offered valuable insight about how the enemy moved and interacted with the civilian populations—in our case, the civilians of Song Mao.

I took one look at the panic-stricken faces of the surviving ARVN soldiers and knew in my gut that this day was not going to end well. *Shit!* Both ARVN soldiers spoke at record speed to our scout as they gestured with chaotic arm movements. It took our scout several minutes to calm them down.

Captain Hudson gleaned as much information as he could from the South Vietnamese soldiers. Then he held a meeting with his company lieutenants and platoon sergeants. When Lt. Anderson returned, I could feel the blood drain from my face as he said, "Radio check the other RTOs in Charlie Company. We are going to have a look-see at the ambush site."

Sgt. Porter once told me that our battalion commander put continual pressure on Charlie Company to produce more body count, a term I had not heard before. Vietnam was a war of attrition: a military strategy in which a belligerent side attempts to win a war by wearing down its enemy to the point of collapse through continuous losses in personnel and material. In preparation to set out, I surmised that Captain Hudson and his lieutenant platoon leaders saw this as an excellent opportunity to add an increased enemy body count to their resumes, and in the process, perhaps earn a few citations.

After the ARVN interrogation, Charlie Company saddled up and moved out with care to gather intelligence and police the battlefield, as they put it. Within thirty minutes, we heard the first enemy sniper fire. Sgt. Porter determined the type of rifle being fired as a Browning Automatic Rifle (BAR), signaling an enemy insurgent Viet Cong. NVA soldiers were equipped with Russian made AK-47s that made a distinct popping sound when fired.

We returned fire in the direction of the sniper, who was probably hiding in a tree, or maybe a spider hole. Every man in Charlie Company lay prone on the jungle floor until given the command to move out. Several minutes later the sniper fire resumed and nailed Mendoza, a soldier in First Platoon.

"Jesus, God! I'm hit! I'm hit in the neck! MEDIC!"

We lay frozen on the jungle floor while Mendoza screamed. The sniper had hidden well and would pick off anyone who moved toward Mendoza. Lt. Anderson switched the PRC radio to command net. He grabbed the handset of the radio and squeezed the transmit bar.

"Panther One, this is Dragon Lady Two. Do you copy? Over."

"Copy, Dragon Lady."

I recognized the voice of our CO, Captain Hudson, who was several meters to our rear.

"This is Panther One," the CO said. "What is your situation, Dragon Lady? Over."

"We have a man down from First Platoon, a bullet injury to his neck, hopefully a graze. Over," Lt. Anderson said. "Sniper fire coming from a position fifty meters to our front. Request artillery fire."

Lt. Anderson unfolded his topo map and provided coordinates to Captain Hudson, hoping that artillery shells would not land too close to friendlies.

"Roger that, Dragon Lady Two," Captain Hudson said. "Sending Willie Peter marker rounds to your coordinates." Willie Peter was code for white phosphorous. WP rounds could be deadly if they landed too close to friendlies. When a shell landed, it would shoot up little sparks of white phosphorous, a chemical that burned without needing oxygen. If it landed on you, it burned right through your skin down to the bone. On the plus side, WP made thick white smoke that would provide Lt. Anderson excellent sightings to adjust his artillery coordinates.

From out of nowhere, I heard a whooshing sound followed by a bright white flash a good forty meters to our front. White smoke billowed up from the jungle floor.

Lt. Anderson squeezed the transmit bar on the PRC. "Add ten, Panther One. Over."

I heard a dull boom to our rear followed by more whooshing sounds above the jungle canopy as 105 mm artillery shells rained down on the enemy that propelled large chunks of shrapnel slashing through the surrounding trees and vegetation. More salvos of artillery continued until Lt. Anderson got on the horn and called, "Cease fire. Over."

Two soldiers from First Platoon rushed to Mendoza's aid and carried him to a Dust Off position one klick to our rear. He was loaded onto a medevac chopper and flown to a nearby field hospital in Nha Trang. Moments later, Charlie Company saddled up to continue our slow trek to the ARVN ambush site.

Chapter Nineteen

Baptism by Fire

Forty-five minutes later, Charlie Company encountered the clatter of small arms fire: AK-47s, BARs, rocket-propelled grenades, and the roar of .51 caliber machine guns, followed by the popping sound of enemy mortar tubes.

We had walked into an enemy ambush, and the VC and NVA were unleashing a barrage of ear-hammering firepower in our direction. AK-47 bullets cracked overhead snapping branches off trees. Bark, leaves, dust, dirt, and other debris rained down on us as we burrowed into the jungle floor.

We wasted no time returning fire with M 14s and M16s rifles, M60s, and thumpers, our M79 grenade launchers firing 40 x 46 mm grenades. Our machine gunner in Second Platoon, Sgt. Roach, blew past Lt. Anderson and me, followed by his two ammo bearers. Roach got into position on the right flank where he would not be firing on any friendlies and in a practiced motion, propped his gun on a tripod. He opened up with his M60 machine gun, shell casings flying in every direction as he swiveled his gun 30 degrees, left to right, destroying anything in its path.

Once again, Lt. Anderson called in artillery on the PRC-25. We had no time for WP markers as we were getting hammered with gunfire from enemy soldiers. My ear drums felt pummeled by the concussive, ear-deafening exchange of intense rifle fire, yet I thought I heard Lt. Anderson request an air strike on the VC and NVA regulars. If he had, I hoped the jets would drop bombs and not napalm.

The raging storm of gunfire continued for several minutes. Lt. Anderson radioed First Platoon commander, Lt. Campbell, to get a situation report. Campbell's platoon was walking point and probably had several casualties.

"Bamboo Viper One, this is Dragon Lady Two," Lt. Anderson yelled over the cacophony. "Do you copy? Over."

Lt. Campbell's shaky voice came through the noise. "Copy that, Dragon Lady. We are in deep shit here. Walked right into an NVA ambush. VC insurgents, probably company size, maybe bigger. I have five confirmed KIAs and several wounded. We need help here, Dragon Lady; artillery or an air strike so we can retreat. Over."

"Copy that, Bamboo Viper," said Lt. Anderson. "Calling in more artillery and requesting an air strike. When those shells start hitting the NVA, pull out to your rear position. We will try and give you cover on the flanks. Call me if those shells are hitting too close. Over."

"Copy that, Dragon Lady. Over."

In moments, we heard a thunderous barrage of projectiles whooshing overhead from a different artillery battery to our rear. The shells were coming from a huge 175 mm howitzer that had a firing range of twenty-five miles and could inflict a wider range of damage on the enemy compared to the previous 105 mm shells. The bombardment continued for several minutes as 175 mm shells rained down on the enemy, the ground trembling like an earthquake with every explosion.

I heard Lt. Campbell's voice come through the hiss of the radio.

"Dragon Lady Two, this is Bamboo Viper One. Artillery target is dead on. Enemy fire has ceased. Pulling back now from our position, please cease fire. Over."

"CEASE FIRE!" Lt. Anderson yelled loud enough for all to hear.

Seconds later, soldiers from First Platoon retreated past Second Platoon to a position at our rear; some men carrying the wounded, others carrying the dead. I saw soldiers with bloody bandages attached to their heads dragging other wounded soldiers to a safe place behind a tree or anthill where a medic could attend to their wounds.

"Okay, Private Madigan," Lt Anderson said. "I'm going to count to three. And on three, we both jump up and retreat to a safer position. Huey gunships should be arriving any second, and they will be raking the area with rockets and 40 mm gunfire. We want to give them a clear field of fire."

On "three" we jumped up and retreated. An object sailed past my head, and to my horror, saw it was a Chicom, a crudely manufactured Chinese hand grenade that landed three meters in front of me and the L-T.

My training from Tigerland kicked in. I ran past the grenade at a 30 degree right angle and turned my body so I would take shrapnel on my flank when it detonated. Lt. Anderson followed suit and ran at a 30 degree left angle. We blew past the grenade, maybe three or four meters, when it detonated. The explosion shattered the air and the concussion rocked me forward another three meters. The impact knocked the rifle out of my hands as my body hit the ground.

My lungs felt robbed of oxygen and my first reaction was to gulp air. I thought I was going to die from not being able to breathe. I felt as if the life force had been sucked out of my body along with my breath. I had the wind knocked out of me once as a catcher in Little League and doubled over then. Now I wondered if I would survive the intensity of this experience.

Soldiers near me were hit by the same grenade. "MEDIC!" They screamed in unison. I had no idea if I had taken shrapnel from the grenade or otherwise injured myself like I had the first time when I lost a chunk of my leg.

Minutes later, I was able to catch my breath. Dazed, and with my ears ringing from the explosion, I looked around to assess my situation. I saw Lt. Anderson lying still in a shallow ravine to my left. My heart raced, but I heard him groan and took a deep breath, knowing he had survived the impact.

As I came more into my own awareness, I felt pain in my upper left hip and saw my bloodied fatigue pants, a thickening burgundy stain from my waist down to my thigh. Pain set in as I examined the extent of the blood where it soaked toward the ground. I guessed I had taken shrapnel there. My back had been protected from the blast by angling my body, and also from the bulk of the PRC-25 radio.

Overall, I felt a sense of relief for having survived the firefight and enemy grenade. I low crawled, relying on my forearms and one good leg, to a position of cover behind a large anthill. It was the first time I was thankful for the multitudes of insects in Vietnam, but this was no time to rest. I sensed the VC and NVA would soon advance on our position.

Moments later, the jungle exploded with automatic weapons fire. The VC and NVA had indeed advanced their positions. Every boonie rat in Charlie Company hit the dirt and they returned fire on the enemy with M16s and M60s. The distinctive *pop-pop-pop* of the Russian made AK-47 kicked up small puffs of dirt near my anthill.

Motherfuckin' dinks are trying to finish me off, I thought. *Why are these people trying to kill me? Fuck this shit! I'm not going down without a fight!*

I felt helpless without a rifle. Behind me I heard wounded soldiers screaming in pain: "MEDIC! MEDIC!" Then I heard the familiar *whoop-whoop-whoop* of incoming helicopters. Two Cobra gunships equipped with the latest armaments flew in low.

The Cobra, aka the Snake, was a narrow Air Cav assault helicopter that carried the pilot and gunner in tandem. The gunner operated a mini-gun, an electrically operated Gatling gun with six barrels. The bird was also equipped with a belt-fed M75 40 mm grenade launcher attached to its nose, and the undercarriage housed a cylindrical tube that fired nineteen wire-guided 2.75 inch rockets. Both gunships opened up with a fusillade of metal and rockets that showered down on the enemy position and provided a momentary respite from enemy fire.

I took inventory of my wounds, and through my tattered pants, I could see a mushy area where shrapnel had hit. Blood continued to drain out of my wounds faster than I imagined, drenching my pant leg. My left hip/buttock area needed attention by a medic, and fast, or I would succumb to blood loss. I did not want to pass out, left to die on the rotting jungle floor.

I had to stay focused. A blaze of enemy gunfire erupted from a tree line twenty meters to the left of my forward position. It was a Russian-made .51 caliber machine gun, its rounds stitching through the ground on either side of the anthill. Thank God the hill was wide enough to provide good cover. Though I could not retrieve my rifle, I still had all five M26 fragmentation grenades attached to my web gear.

I detached the grenades and laid them on the ground in front of me. I took a chance and peeked around the anthill. Yellow muzzle fire from the .51 caliber machine gun erupted from the tree line. Then the firing stopped. An enemy soldier poked his head up—I could see his pith helmet—and he parted a few shrubby branches. Then he stood up, parted a few more branches for a better look at my position. I saw his face and the top of his mustard-colored uniform: an NVA soldier. For an instant we stared at each other. I had never actually seen an enemy NVA and here we were with our eyes locked, face to face, albeit at a short distance. I darted back.

I had not cooked off a grenade since my stint at Tigerland. During infantry training, two drill sergeants gave a demonstration on how many times a grenade can go back and forth in five seconds. The two men were in foxholes fifteen meters apart, and the demonstration grenade had a charge inside that popped like a firecracker after five seconds. The grenade sailed back and forth between foxholes at least three times before it detonated.

I pulled the pin on my first grenade, let the handle fly off, which started the charge, and counted: *one thousand…two thousand…three thousand….* I poked my head around the anthill and lobbed the grenade at the machine gun position. The grenade had enough momentum to land at the base and roll forward into the enemy foxhole. The explosion was muffled, which meant it rolled into the depression past the tree line and hit my target.

I breathed a sigh of relief and thought for the first time that day, maybe, just maybe, I could make it out alive. Even though I was bleeding out, I had never felt so alive in my life.

I repeated cooking off the rest of the grenades in the same fashion every time I detected muzzle fire from the enemy. I may have left my rifle behind, but it felt good bringing the damn damn down on the VC and NVA. I figured I had taken out one, and possibly two enemy machine gun nests.

Pain in my left hip worsened as it shot through my body and into my lower extremities. Every moment I lay behind the anthill, I lost more blood. I needed a medic if I was to survive. I reached into the top pocket of my shirt and pulled out the rosary my mother had given me the day I left Los Angeles for Vietnam. I never went into a combat mission without it. My chances for survival grew slim and I decided to make my peace with God.

I was halfway through an Act of Contrition when I heard a scuffling sound behind me. I turned with a start. Sgt. Porter pulled himself toward me in a low crawl. When he got close enough, he grabbed the web gear attached to my shoulders and whispered, "Hold on, buddy. I'm going to drag you out of here."

And he did. Porter dragged me backward across the jungle floor, using my web gear as a convenient handle while soldiers from Second Platoon opened up with suppressive automatic gunfire to give us cover. We got to a safe position in a depression behind a copse of teak trees. He removed his fatigue shirt and made a tourniquet above my left thigh in an effort to stop the bleeding from the jagged, baseball-sized piece of shrapnel embedded in my flesh. Next, he handed me his .45 pistol and a few magazines and took off to find Lt. Anderson.

Chapter Twenty-One

Dust Off

An eerie silence I didn't trust hovered over the battlefield. The air didn't stir, and I tried to stay alert while waiting for Sgt. Porter to return with Lt. Anderson. Branches snapped and I heard leaves rustling five meters to my front. I figured a sapper was inching close to finish me off. I pointed my .45 in the direction of the sound. I froze until I heard a familiar voice.

"Put that piece down, Private, before I scatter your shit to the wind."

I scanned the area in front of me until I recognized a crouching figure; it was Specialist 4th Class Angelo Martinez, our Second Platoon medic. He had done a good job of camouflaging himself in the foliage a mere few meters in front of me. He prided himself on his technique and he blended in seamlessly with the vegetation, almost invisible had he not spoken.

"Where's Sgt. Porter?" Martinez asked.

"He went out to find Lt. Anderson and drag him back to safety like he did with me," I answered. "Man, am I ever glad to see you, Specialist. I got hit with shrapnel from a Chicom and I'm bleeding everywhere. And it's starting to fucking hurt bad."

Martinez unfastened his web gear and took out his M-5 medical kit. He laid a green towel on the jungle floor, recreating a scene familiar to me only weeks before. He used the scissors to cut open my fatigues near my left hip and examined the flesh wound.

"Looks worse than it is," Martinez said. "You took a nice chunk in your hip, Madigan. I'm going to patch you up until we can get your ass to a Dust Off site."

He cleaned the wound, first with water and a clean towel, and then with a dousing of alcohol, which stung like hell on fire, but I was thankful for the attention. He pulled out several large bandages from his kit, applied a few to the wound hole and taped them off. Next, he took out a syrette of morphine and injected the hypodermic needle in an area above my left thigh. He examined my left knee and right ankle; both had taken smaller fragments. He ignored other tiny bits that were not a threat.

"The wounds in your lower legs have stopped bleeding. You will be fine until we can get you to a field hospital," Martinez said. "For now, let's sit tight and wait for Sgt. Porter. Captain Hudson called in for a Dust Off about half a klick to our rear. Most of the wounded are being medevaced out of this shithole. But we aren't leaving until Sgt. Porter returns."

Minutes later, we heard a rustling sound. Sgt. Porter appeared from the brush and dragged Lt. Anderson to our spot behind the teak trees. Martinez attended to Lt. Anderson who was semi-conscious and moaning in a low drawl.

"Same wounds as yours, Madigan," Martinez said, "only the opposite side. Concussion from the grenade knocked him unconscious, but I think he will come around soon."

Once again, a barrage of enemy gunfire erupted from the tree line twenty meters to our front. And once again, bullets whizzed over our heads like a swarm of angry bees. Sgt. Porter had an M60, but no tripod for the heavy M60 machine gun. Several bandoleers of ammo were attached to the lieutenant's web gear. Porter braced himself against a teak tree, put the butt of the gun against his hip and began spraying suppressive automatic gunfire at the tree line. Martinez assisted him by feeding belts of 7.62 full metal jackets into Porter's weapon.

I watched the ensuing battle through a film of morphine. Sgt. Porter yelled something I didn't understand as he fired his weapon at the VC and NVA soldiers. He grinned ear to ear as he blasted away.

Oh my God! I thought. *He's actually enjoying this.*

Porter paused as Martinez gathered more belts of ammo. He saw me looking at him in stoned wonder.

"MADIGAN!" He tried to yell above the racket. "WELCOME TO THE WIDE WORLD OF WAR!"

Sweet Jesus, Sgt. Porter has turned into a madman!

I heard the radio as it crackled to life. "Dragon Lady Two, this is Panther One. Do you copy? Over."

It was our CO, Captain Hudson. Porter went for the handset and keyed the transmit bar. "Panther One, this is Dragon Lady Two. I copy. Over."

Captain Hudson requested a situation report. Sgt. Porter complied. Hudson gave Porter topo map coordinates of the Dust Off position to our rear and instructed him to retreat with Martinez and his two wounded soldiers as soon as he felt it was safe.

"Copy that, Panther One. Over," Porter said. He handed me the transmit bar. "Can't believe that Prick-25 still works after getting riddled with shrapnel from that Chicom," he chuckled.

I was also amazed, but when silence proceeded his laugh, the air felt heavy and I had another sense of foreboding. It was too quiet.

We heard a muted boom in the distance followed by an ever-increasing roar.

"Holy shit!" Martinez said to Porter. "What do you think, Sarge? More artillery?"

Porter held his hand up to quiet Martinez and stared at an opening above us in the jungle canopy. He closed his eyes and assumed a deep state of concentration. As the roar grew in intensity, a little smile formed on Porter's face.

"I'LL TELL YOU WHAT," Porter screamed as the roar now became ear-splitting. "THAT AIN'T NO FUCKIN' ARTILLERY!"

Porter, Martinez, and I looked up through the opening in the jungle canopy as two Air Force F-4 Phantom II jet fighter-bombers flashed overhead, their silver underbellies glinting in the afternoon sun. Both aircraft were flying at supersonic speed and had caused the muffled boom we heard moments earlier. Coming in low from the east, they flew above the treetops, so close we could feel the heat from the jets' exhaust washing down on us, and the turbojet engines vibration shaking the trees and earth. I had never heard a sweeter sound in my life.

"Dragon Lady Two, this is Night Hawk Three. Do you copy? Over."

I looked at Sgt. Porter and said, "I, uh, forgot to tell you, Sergeant. Lt. Anderson called in an air strike after we got pinned down."

Porter grimaced and grabbed the handset. "Night Hawk Three, this is Dragon Lady Two. I copy. Over."

Both jets circled above our position performing figure eights at three thousand feet while waiting for Porter's reply. They were also letting the VC and NVA soldiers know that this day was not going to end well for them.

"Dragon Lady Two," the lead pilot said, "I'm going to need a sitrep and coordinates of your current position. Over."

"Copy that, Night Hawk," Sgt. Porter replied. He pulled out his topo map and compass, studied the grid coordinates and relayed our position to the pilot with pinpoint accuracy.

"Affirmative, Dragon Lady," the pilot said. "Here's the plan; I will make the first pass firing 20 mike mikes as a marker in front of your coordinates. Please make any corrections. Second pass will be a bombing raid. Are you equipped with smoke grenades?"

I tugged on Sgt. Porter's arm and held up two fingers as I remembered I had attached two smoke grenades to my web gear before the Mini-Cav mission started. "Yellow and purple," I said to Porter.

"Affirmative, Night Hawk. Two smokes, one yellow, one purple. Over."

"Roger, Dragon Lady. I will be making my descent from your south, southeast. When I reach an elevation of five hundred feet, pop the yellow smoke. Over."

"Mike mikes?" Martinez asked. "What the hell?"

"He'll be firing 20 millimeter rockets as a marker before the bombing raid," Porter said. "Then I can make any corrections. After those fast-movers come in on their bombing raid, we'll *didi* out of here to Dust Off."

"Madigan," Porter said, "how are you holding up?"

"I'm okay, Sarge."

The syrette of morphine had eased the pain in my hips and legs, and I felt confident about being able to get back to Dust Off as quickly as possible, with the help, of course, of the two F-4 jets and Specialist Martinez.

We heard the whine of the lead jet as it made its descent from three thousand feet. As the pilot approached our position, I felt as if I had been lying beneath a moving freight train. If it hadn't been that loud, I wondered if I was going deaf. From a crouch, I plugged my ears with my hands and opened my mouth. The jungle floor shook worse than before as the F-4 jets descended to five hundred feet and screeched above the jungle canopy.

Sgt. Porter popped the yellow smoke grenade and heaved it toward the tree line that camouflaged the VC and NVA bunkers. The fighter-bomber jet fired a burst of 20 mm rockets from its underbelly, strafing trees and vegetation twenty to thirty meters forward of the billowing yellow smoke. Then the F-4 pulled up hard right sweeping in a great arc as he ascended to join the other jet at three thousand feet.

Porter keyed the transmit bar on the radio. "Night Hawk Three, this is Dragon Lady. Left forward, five meters. Over," Porter said.

"Roger that, Dragon Lady," the pilot said, confirming the corrections. "Next pass will be the bombing raid. Keep your heads down. Try and evac after my pass. Over."

"Copy that, Night Hawk. Over."

We heard the high pitched whine of the F-4s as they began their descent. Porter popped the purple smoke grenade and tossed it in the same area as the yellow.

"Okay," Porter said. "Get ready to move out after those fast movers drop their payload. The enemy will be digging in deep as those jets get close. I've got the L-T. Martinez, you grab Madigan. Keep your heads down and move at a steady pace to Dust Off."

Both F-4s came streaking in at 430 knots, flying seventy feet above the treetops. I said a silent prayer. *Please God, keep those jets on the right heading and blast those motherfuckers to kingdom come.*

As the first jet thundered overhead, I looked up and saw the F-4 release a cluster of 250-pound projectiles; the bombs sprouted fins to slow their descent and gave the pilot time to pull out before the explosions. My eardrums seemed to scream at me from inside my head as the bombs found their target. Shockwaves from the blasts reverberated in ever-widening concentric circles across the jungle floor, giving me the sensation of being at the base of an erupting volcano.

Seconds later, the second jet came screaming in low and repeated the discharge of cluster bombs on the enemy target. When the dust cleared, Porter stood and wrapped Lt. Anderson's arms around his shoulders. "OKAY, BOONIE RATS," he shouted. "TIME TO *DIDI!*"

Martinez helped me up. He prompted me to wrap my left arm around his neck, and using my good-enough right leg, we hobbled off in retreat to Dust Off.

Chapter Twenty-Two

Red Badge

I felt grateful that the F-4 fighter-bombers did a good job flattening the Viet Cong and North Vietnamese Army bunkers, and we did not experience enemy fire during our withdrawal.

As we approached Dust Off, I heard loud blasts coming from the area and thought, *Oh shit! The site is being mortared!* Then I saw the explosions were coming from an Air Cav corps of engineers who were wrapping det cord, a cordlike explosive, around the base of trees to widen the area so more medevac choppers could land and evacuate the dead and wounded.

The medevac Slicks, were marked with a large red cross on the nose and both sides of the chopper, and they were coming in swiftly, three at a time.

Martinez dragged me to an incoming bird. He stood on the skids and hoisted me up to another medic, who had just spread ponchos over three dead soldiers. The medic pulled me in and laid me sprawled out over the ponchos. Martinez jumped aboard, pulled out another syringe of morphine from his medical bag, and injected me in my left thigh. I felt the effects of the drug reduce my sense of pain. And like the first time I received morphine for my previous wound, I felt both emotional and chatty.

I didn't let the fact that Martinez was scrawling notes on my forehead stop me, and I grasped his arm. "Specialist Martinez, I need to tell you something important, very important!"

Martinez smiled at my maudlin affect. He finished scribbling notes on my forehead for the medics back at the MASH unit in Phan Thiêt. "Okay, Madigan, lay it on me. And by the way, you can call me Angel from here on out. You earned that today, my friend."

The morphine continued to take effect and I felt no pain. "Specialist Martinez, um, Angel. Today I saw the elephant…nose to nose… eyeball to eyeball…and I wasted the fucker!"

Martinez nodded in understanding. He stored his marking pencil back in his kit, leaned forward, and kissed me on the forehead. "Yes, you certainly did see the elephant, my friend, and you will receive a Purple Heart for your actions, maybe even a Bronze Star. Today you went through your baptism of fire. I was pinned down by AK fire, but I watched you cook off those fragmentation grenades. I'm sure you took out one or two machine gun nests. You proved yourself to be a good soldier today when the shit hit the fan."

The medevac pilot pointed his index finger skyward, indicating to Martinez that he would be lifting off. The chopper had been loaded with dead and wounded, and was ready to return to a field hospital in Phan Thiêt.

Martinez jumped off the bird. He needed to attend to more wounded soldiers entering the Dust Off site. "Take good care of yourself, Madigan," Martinez yelled as the chopper began to lift. "Judging by that hole in your hip, you won't be seeing combat for at least three, maybe four months. I have twelve days and a wake-up. Maybe I will see you again in the states someday."

I waved back to Angel feeling overcome with love for that soldier, for Sgt. Porter, and every soldier in Charlie Company who fought so hard and valiantly that day against a well-armed and tenacious enemy. I felt love in my heart for the brave F-4 pilots whose bombing raid provided a safe escape to Dust Off and, in turn, probably saved our lives.

I experienced a smooth takeoff while the medevac helicopter ascended rapidly. That changed when it banked hard, and flew in a zig-zag pattern to avoid being hit by enemy ground fire. We headed southwest toward Phan Thiêt, and each time the chopper banked, the dead soldiers under me shifted with the turbulence.

In my discomfort, several thoughts flooded my brain. Foremost, I was thankful to be alive. I was sure I would pull through with proper medical attention at the field hospital in Phan Thiêt. I imagined the type of care I would receive once we landed, so different than the men beneath me for whom it was too late.

I looked down at my hip and bloody fatigue pants and thought about my high school vice principle, Father Lopez, a Dominican priest. Father Lopez was also the librarian at St. John Vianney. I was often assigned to work in the library when I reported for three o'clock detention. I was a freshman and still reading comic books and the Hardy Boys. Father Lopez took an interest in me and decided it was time to wean me off those juvenile reads. He suggested Hemingway short stories that featured a character named Nick Adams. I found new interest in these life-and-death tales with titles such as "Indian Camp" and "Big Two-Hearted River."

What really came to mind was the first novel Father Lopez presented to me: *The Red Badge of Courage*. This novel by Stephen Crane relates the story of Henry Fleming, a teenager who enlists in the Union Army during the Civil War. Henry has hopes of fulfilling his dreams of glory. The "red badge" was literally a bloody wound soldiers received in war, and metaphorically signaled courage.

Looking at my "red badge," I thought how prescient Father Lopez had been in recommending that book as my first high school read.

Like the protagonist, Henry Fleming, I harbored dreams of being a valiant and brave soldier; that is, until my first Search and Destroy mission where reality set in. I witnessed the horror of the wounded and dead bodies scattered on the battlefield. Unlike Henry, I decided to give myself a daily reminder: I was a well-trained infantry soldier. Belief and faith in myself helped me keep sharp focus and stay hyper-aware of my surroundings. Maybe, just maybe, I would make it through this awful war—one day at a time. "Stay alert. Stay alive," became my daily mantra.

Forty minutes after liftoff, the medevac chopper began its descent as it approached the airstrip at LZ Betty. I saw several tight groups of soldiers as they stood off the runway, waiting, as a whole lineup of medevac choppers followed to our rear. Some of the soldiers held collapsible gurneys and stretchers for the wounded; others held body bags for the KIAs.

When my chopper landed, soldiers gathered on either side and unloaded the wounded first. I was placed on a stretcher, and inspected by a field hospital medic who directed that I be placed in a secure area off the airstrip with grunts who sustained less critical wounds. The severely wounded were placed on wheeled gurneys and rushed into the nearby field hospital.

One thing I noticed was how many FNGs had been deployed to help with the unloading. They stood out because of their fresh, green fatigues, shiny boots and the blank look on their faces. I guessed these fuckin' new guys, hence FNGs, had arrived at LZ Betty in the past few days, and were getting an unwelcome preview of what awaited them in the bush. Vietnam was unique in that individual troops were rotated in and out in twelve-month tours. I looked at the worried faces of these FNGs and realized that only two months before, I was one of those guys. It seemed like a lifetime ago.

When Caswell, Kent, and I were assigned to Second Platoon of Charlie Company in early February, I overheard Specialist Martinez say to Sgt. Porter, "These guys are still shitting stateside chow."

An FNG had a higher attrition rate than experienced troops, and was often shunned or scorned until he passed that magic, unseen line to respectability. For me, that happened early on my first Search and Destroy mission when I held my own as we encountered the enemy in several firefights. My infantry training at Tigerland and my natural instinct to stay alive kicked in on my first combat mission.

On my gurney, I watched the lineup of medevac birds land and unload the dead and wounded. Without thinking, I reached into the top pocket of my fatigue shirt and pulled out my rosary. I thanked God that I had survived this day and prayed for all the brave men in Charlie Company. Then I prayed for a safe and speedy recovery.

Chapter Twenty-Three

Nha Trang

I left the mess hall at 2:30 p.m., having spun my true tales to an appreciative audience, and once again found my favorite spot in the tea garden. The wind had died down and the Bay of Tokyo mirrored the azure-blue sky above. The sun glittered on the water's surface, creating thousands of tiny sparkles. The scent of cherry blossoms filled the air and the sound of trickling water into the pond quieted my mind into a peaceful meditative state.

I felt transformed, as if the everyday scenes of life had taken on an exaggerated beauty I appreciated anew: the cherry blossoms with their delicate pink flowers basking in the sunlight, the gorgeous well-manicured sunken gardens, the cluster of wisteria and dwarf pines in the tea garden. I had seen pretty flowers in the states, but had I really seen them? Like this? I knew it had something to do with seeing the elephant. Maybe everything.

Every second felt like a prayer of supreme gratitude for having come out of the ambush at Song Mao. I know I felt that way when I woke up in a bed with clean sheets in the 8th Field Hospital in Nha Trang. Randy Kent, my fellow boonie rat in Charlie Company, was also wounded in Song Mao and ended up in a bed right across from me. I was glad he was there too.

On my second day at Nha Trang, I was wheeled on a gurney into an operating room. The head surgeon greeted me with a warm sense of assurance. He said I was about to get a shot, and to count backward from one hundred after the needle was pulled from my spine.

"We're going to try for the larger pieces of shrapnel lodged in your left hip and lower legs," he said. "Don't worry, Private Madigan, you'll be knocked out enough with this spinal anesthetic; that is, you won't feel a thing during the operation."

I probably counted backward to eighty-nine or eighty-eight when the drug started to take effect; I felt the nurse put a breathing mask on my face as I began to pass out. I awoke several hours later in a recovery room along with a few other patients. I felt dull pain in my left hip/buttock area, my left knee, and my right ankle. I wondered if the surgeon was able to extract all the enemy shrapnel from my body. I wiggled my fingers and toes and felt relief that everything still worked.

Then I started praying, thanking God for being there with me and getting me to safety after surviving that awful NVA ambush. A nurse came by my bed and seeing me awake, handed me a small paper cup of water and another cup with two red pills.

"Take these pills, Private Madigan, and wash them down with water," she said. "They will help alleviate the pain. Your surgery was successful and you will be good as new in a few months. Maybe a scar here and there, but they will eventually disappear with time."

I didn't know if that was good news or bad news. I certainly wanted to heal properly, but I wasn't looking forward to humping in the bush again. A few hours later I was wheeled back to my bed in the main ward. Across the aisle, I saw Randy Kent asleep. He had also undergone surgery. His left hand and both arms were wrapped in fresh dressings. Both of us had escaped major injuries that fateful day in the field.

"Attention!" A shoulder shouted.

I looked up, stunned. General William C. Westmoreland, Commander of all United State Forces in Vietnam, walked into our ward followed by a few staff members. One of them carried a Land camera to document the event in photos.

Westmoreland was strikingly handsome with a strong jawline and an air of purposeful confidence. He wore faded but perfectly starched and ironed fatigues with four shiny stars attached to the collars; his boots were also well-shined. In essence, he was a textbook version of how a self-assured Army general should look. Westmoreland had come to present Purple Hearts to every soldier wounded in the ambush at Song Mao.

He approached my bed. "Madigan, huh? Sounds like an Irishman to me," he quipped. He attached the Purple Heart to my pajama top and said, "Thank you, son, for your courage on the battlefield."

His staff member snapped a picture of me wearing the heart and handed me the Polaroid photo; a memento I knew I would always treasure.

Westmoreland continued, "How are you doing, Madigan?"

"Fine, sir," I replied. "Just a toothache compared to most of these guys. I'll be fine, General."

He smiled, shook my hand, and moved to the next bed.

. . .

In time, I was able to hobble about on crutches. I liked to join Kent for a smoke break on an outside patio area adjacent to our ward. Smoking was prohibited in the hospital. Randy and I enjoyed getting out into fresh air, sitting at one of the small tables, and lighting up.

We avoided talking about the war. Instead, we talked about how we would be surfing, drinking beer, and chasing girls when we got back to The World. The only drawback of sitting outside was the one-story building next door that hummed from several compressors that ran all day and night. To compensate, we had to speak a bit louder. I figured it was some kind of refrigeration unit that stored meat and other perishables.

One day, a guy named Miller, a medical specialist who assisted the doctors and nurses in the hospital, joined the two of us during our break. We enjoyed his company while we shot the breeze.

A large five-ton 6 x 6 Army truck pulled up to the refrigerated building. The driver's door had a large black cross painted on the side with the initials GR painted below. It struck me as odd since most medical vehicles had a red cross with a white background painted on the side, as did the medevac Dust Off helicopters.

Two soldiers exited the vehicle, opened the rear doors, and pulled out a large double gurney on wheels. They loaded long, dark plastic bags on the gurney. The bags had a zipper running up the center and the word "Head" imprinted on the top.

"*Oh, fuck me!*" Kent cried out. "Those are fucking body bags, Walt! That building must be a refrigeration unit to temporarily store the bodies."

Specialist Miller looked nonplussed. He took a drag on his cigarette and chimed in. "That's right, guys. GR stands for Graves Registration. In that building the dead soldiers are identified by their dog tags or maybe wallet identification, sometimes just a letter from home. Then they clean up the bodies, they're embalmed, tagged and bagged, and put into tin coffins. Next they're shipped off to Ton Son Nhut airport by Saigon—or as we call it The KIA Travel Bureau—where they will be loaded up on Air Force cargo planes and flown back to the States to be claimed by their families for a funeral and proper burial."

It took several minutes for Miller's words to sink in. Kent and I sat there in respectful silence as we watched the GR soldiers do their job. I would rather be a grunt out humping in the bush any day of the week than have that gruesome assignment. I never gave much thought to what happened to soldiers once they were killed in combat—too depressing. I put my full concentration on staying alive during our Search and Destroy missions. The GR soldiers must have transferred at least forty bodies before they jumped back in the truck and departed.

Kent and I looked at each other, knowing we were thinking the same thing: *that could easily have been one of us in those body bags.*

"Jesus, Madigan," Kent said. "Do you think any of those bodies belonged to Charlie Company? I remember hearing of at least 5 KIAs in that ambush, maybe more."

"I don't know, and I don't think I want to know," I said. "Do you realize how fucking lucky we are to have survived that ambush with relatively minor wounds? Did I tell you Sgt. Porter low crawled to my position where several dinks from that tree line were trying to punch my ticket? Fuckin' slopes wanted me dead, man. Then those fast movers arrived to save the day. Otherwise, I would be in one of those body bags."

Chapter Twenty-Four

Catholic School Days

Sitting in the tea garden, I had a little less than two hours before I had to return to the barracks in Building C. The late afternoon sun cast long shadows as it descended westward. I stood up from my bench, stretched, and decided to take a short walk to unkink my legs.

Dappled sunlight filtered through the cherry blossom trees that cast a pinkish glow on the pond, and the wind picked up again, creating white-edged wavelets on Tokyo Bay. My inner self, though calm, had not lost that wonderful feeling of elation. I thought about my family and what their reaction would be when I called them from Travis Air Force Base in California. I was especially close to my two older sisters, Maureen and Kathleen, two and four years older, respectively.

I was born into a blue-collar, working-class, Irish Catholic family, the sixth of eight kids. Money always seemed to be an issue with my parents. Despite their financial concerns, my mother made darn sure we all had a Catholic education from first through twelfth grade. After that, we were on our own.

Midway through third grade, I was recruited by Father Mullins, the pastor of my parochial school, Holy Spirit, to begin training as an altar boy. I had strong religious convictions and never missed Sunday Mass unless I was deathly ill, and even then, I would still try and attend.

Sunday Mass is based on the fourth commandment: "Remember the Sabbath day to keep it holy." To deliberately miss Sunday Mass without just reason would objectively be considered a mortal sin. And if, by chance, I were to die in a state of mortal sin, having not gone to confession, I would immediately bypass purgatory and go straight to hell—and not pass Go and collect $200.

And so it came to pass that my older sisters, Kathy and Maureen, woke me up in a panic one Sunday after setting the clocks ahead two hours, and informed me I had overslept and missed the twelve noon Mass, the last of the day.

"Oh, no!" I cried, "I need to get to confession immediately!"

"No you don't," Kathy said. "You're in luck; I'm going to conduct Mass in our living room. Maureen will assist me as an altar girl. Go in the living room and sit on the couch. Mass will begin in five minutes."

I sat on the couch and wondered where my mother was as I knew she always attended Mass at ten-thirty.

My two sisters created an altar consisting of two end tables stacked on top of each other and covered with a sheet adorned with several tiny plastic crosses. On top of the altar was a chalice Kathy had borrowed from my mother's silver collection. A missal lay next to it. At the base of the altar were two small clear crystal bottles, one filled with water, the other filled with what appeared to be grape juice.

Five minutes later I heard a bell tingle as Kathy and Maureen entered the living room. Maureen carried a wooden pole with a crucifix attached at the top. It looked like the same crucifix my mother hung on the wall above her bed. Maureen had on my older brother Kelly's altar boy vestments: an ankle-length red cassock that buttoned down the center. Over that she wore a white linen surplice with a square neck and three-quarter sleeves. In all, she looked the part of an altar girl.

Kathy borrowed one of Neal's black cassocks, but because she did not have a chasuble, an outermost ceremonial garment worn by priests for Sunday Mass, she improvised and created her own. She took a green sheet out of the linen closet and cut a large square hole in the center and wore it over her cassock like a poncho. She used black tape to create a large cross in the center and smaller crosses on the sides. I felt a sigh of relief as Mass commenced, and thought, *maybe I'm not going to hell after all.*

My sisters went through the usual procedures. Kathy raised her hands and recited Latin blessings. When she said, "*Dominus vobiscum* (the Lord be with you)," Maureen recited, "*Et cum spiritu tuo* (and with thy spirit)." Kathy picked up the missal and read the Gospel aloud as I knelt on the carpet, eyes closed, and my hands in prayer. I crossed myself when I finished.

I started to get suspicious when it was time for the Consecration, in which the bread and wine are symbolically transformed into the body and blood of Jesus. I eyed the Communion Eucharist in Kathy's hand. It looked like a flattened piece of Wonder Bread cut into a circle, and the wine sure looked liked the bottled grape juice from the refrigerator.

Kathy approached to deliver Holy Communion; the chalice had been filled with variously colored Communion wafers. I thought that was odd, and then I knew something was terribly wrong when my Communion wafer tasted just like a vanilla Necco.

Our solemn ritual came to a standstill when my mother walked through the front door. Kathy, Maureen and I froze. Mom had a look of shock on her face as she witnessed the bizarre tableau the girls created.

"Kathy! Maureen!"

At least she didn't say my name.

"What in the hell is going on here?"

"Hi, Mom," I said. "I overslept and missed twelve o'clock Mass, so Kathy and Maureen decided to have Mass in the front room."

"Oh, Hell's bells!" She perched her fists on each hip. "Grab your missal," she said to me, "and get off to the twelve o'clock Mass. It's only eleven-thirty. You have plenty of time if you walk fast."

I grabbed the missal off of Kathy's makeshift altar and a couple of Neccos from the chalice, and bolted for the front door. I could hear my mother screaming at my sisters as I stepped off the porch. So much for Sunday Mass in my living room.

This was not the first time Kathy found herself in hot water with my mother. For the most part, Maureen managed to stay off of our mom's radar. However, Kathy was like a homing beacon for trouble in her early teens. Getting caught in her numerous capers and machinations—and paying the price—didn't make a dent in her behavior. Over time, she would earn the moniker "Black Sheep" among us siblings as she always seemed to be the subject of Mom's ire.

My mother was president of the PTA at Holy Spirit. She never learned to drive and walked to the Pico Center three or four times a week to buy groceries. She cooked every night from scratch. We enjoyed a healthy breakfast, a well-packed lunch for school, and a delicious dinner.

One day, when school ended, she and Kathy left together and walked to the Pico Center Market where my mother had a charge account. As they entered the market together, Kathy picked up on a mouth-watering scent and began to wander while our mother shopped in the back of the store. Kathy wanted to know where that wonderful smell originated and followed the scent to the coffee machine where people were putting fresh beans inside to be ground for their home coffee makers. This gave her an idea.

The next day, she took a detour from her walk home and went to the Pico Center Market. She put scoop after scoop of beans into the coffee grinder and made up five bags of ground coffee. She approached the checkout stand looking innocent in her Catholic school uniform, and said to Jack Yura, one of the store's owners, "Please put these bags on my mom's account."

On her journey home, she stopped at various random houses, rang the bell, and gave a pitch. "Hi, I'm selling coffee for a Holy Spirit fundraiser." Then she would sell the coffee grounds for $1.00 or $2.00 depending on the bag's size. Kathy looked adorable in her uniform. People took a shine to her and would invite her in for hot chocolate and cookies.

Kathy could not believe her good fortune and continued her scheme for several days, that is, until my mom received the monthly bill from Pico Center and all hell broke loose. Her coffee caper came to an abrupt end.

Kathy, and her friend, Eileen Murphy, enjoyed playing hopscotch out in front of our house, a harmless activity. They also liked to go to the end of our street where it dead-ended into Ballona Creek. Here they would build forts out of old sheets and timber, and play hide-and-seek, their favorite game.

One weekend while paying hide-and-seek, Kathy and Eileen jumped over a neighbor's fence and discovered a garage that had been converted into a little cottage. It was locked so naturally they tried a side window and were able to pry it open. Once inside, they discovered tables covered with hundreds of new bathing suits of every size, mostly for women and children. Kathy and Eileen were thrilled with their find, and figured no one would ever know they entered the cottage.

They gathered as many suits as they could carry, jumped back over the fence, and yelled, "Olly, olly, oxen free," a phrase that freed them up from the rest of their game, allowing them to hide the bathing suits. They went back to our house on Marvin Avenue and waited until dark to retrieve their booty. They brought the suits back to the closet in Kathy's room.

The next day, Kathy went up the street to share the "Miracle of the Free Bathing Suits" with her girlfriend, Charlene Wolfolk. Intrigued, Charlene and Kathy went to the cottage for another haul. They continued this for a few more days. Kathy took on the role of a female Robinhood and started handing out suits to all the neighbors on our street.

Then one day while making a raid, before you could say "Maiden Mary," the door opened and slammed shut behind them. They turned and to their horror, saw the lady who owned the cottage standing before them. She locked the window and in a menacing voice, told the two girls to put the suits down. She grabbed Kathy's arm and demanded to know her name and where she lived.

Charlene took this opportunity to open the cottage door and bolt for her house. Kathy bit the lady on the hand that held her arm and also managed to escape.

When Kathy got back to our house, she joined Maureen and I on the living room floor where we were watching *The Roy Rogers Show* on TV. We heard a loud knock on the door. Mom answered and to Kathy's dismay, it was the bathing suit lady. The woman yelled in our mother's face, saying her daughter was a thief. She explained she was a subcontractor for a bathing suit company called Rose Marie Reid and what she did when she found out her suits were being pilfered. Kathy crawled across the living room floor in an effort to reach the hallway that led to her bedroom.

"That's her!" The woman pointed at Kathy.

Jim, who was around four years old, walked into the living room to see what all the yelling was about, and to make matters worse, he was wearing a stolen bathing suit.

"And that's one of my suits!" She pointed at Jim.

Mom assured the irate woman that Kathy would go door to door on our street and retrieve every suit if the lady would not press charges. Mom took Jim into the bathroom, removed the suit and returned it to the lady.

Luckily for Kathy, the woman didn't pursue charges. Our dad drove Kathy to Eileen Murphy's house to retrieve the suits they had stolen on the first day. As punishment, Kathy was grounded for several weeks and was not allowed to watch her favorite late afternoon TV show, *American Bandstand*.

Kathy was not the only Madigan who got into trouble. Throughout my tenure at Holy Spirit, I was bestowed the unofficial title of Class Clown because I loved to make comments in the classroom that would make my friends crack up. I craved the adulation of my classmates and loved hearing their laughter, often to the frustration of the nuns teaching the class.

One Friday in the fourth grade, Sister Lawrence marched the class across the schoolyard to the church, which sat on the easternmost section of the property. We were given instructions to go to confession and say our penance at the altar before being dismissed for the day. I had the usual laundry list of sins, mostly venial: I talked back to my mother three times, I fought with my sisters six times, I had impure thoughts, um, twelve times? I had taken notice of female anatomy after Kelly gave me a *Playboy* magazine to read while waiting to get my hair cut the previous week.

After confessing our sins, I knelt at a side altar with my best friend, Fred Benoit, to say our penance in atonement for our misdeeds. I nudged Fred with my left elbow to get his attention. I held my right hand flat, fingers straight, as most did in prayer, and aimed my fingers toward the statue of St. Joseph before us. I gnarled my left hand in a grotesque fashion, as if I had severe arthritis.

Fred gave me a puzzled look.

In a voice loud enough for only Fred to hear, I said, "Please, St. Joseph, please make my hand like the other."

My right hand twisted into a horrible gnarl like my left. Fred tried to hold in his laughter, but he had asthma and let out high-pitched *whoop whoop* sounds followed by uncontrollable laughter.

In seconds, Sister Lawrence rushed up and grabbed us by our uniform collars and dragged us through a side door out of the church.

"Shame on both of you!" Her stern look matched her admonishment. "How dare you laugh and joke in the House of God. Follow me, boys."

She marched us to the convent, part of the Holy Spirit compound, and we spent the next three hours waxing and buffing the hardwood floors as punishment for our sins. I didn't get home that night until after six. When my mother asked where I was, I told her that Fred and I volunteered to wax and buff all the floors at the convent. I stretched the truth a little and decided to leave the gnarled hand incident out of the conversation.

Sister Elizabeth Mary, my sixth grade teacher who was also the school principal, would occasionally treat us to a movie after lunch. She would set up a projector in the Parish Hall where we sat in rows on metal folding chairs.

One day we watched *The Miracle of Our Lady of Fatima*. The film depicted the true life story of three shepherd children who experienced apparitions of the Blessed Virgin Mary, Mother of God, in Portugal in 1917. Lúcia Santos and her two cousins, Jacinta Marto and Francisco Marto, were tending to their flock outside the village of Fatima and praying the Hail Mary when a storm arose. Lightning flashed and a cloud of light surrounded a nearby tree. An apparition of Mary, Mother of God, appeared. She told the children to pray the rosary each day to bring peace to the world and to bring an end to war. At the time, Europe was engaged in World War I. Mother Mary continued to appear on the 13th of each month for the next six months. Then she revealed the three secrets of Fatima to Lúcia, which she kept to herself. Eventually, Lúcia revealed the first two secrets: a vision of hell and a foretelling of the horrors of World War II. The third secret was expected to be revealed by the Pope in the year 2000.

When the film ended, Sister Elizabeth Mary assigned us homework. We were to write down ideas on what the third secret might be for discussion in Religion class the next day.

On the following day, Fred and I were sitting on a bench in the yard outside the school waiting for the bell that signaled the end of our lunch break. Fred divulged a few ideas concerning the third secret and we shared a few laughs.

After entering the classroom, Sister Elizabeth Mary asked if anybody cared to share their ideas on the third secret revealed to Lúcia by Mary, Mother of God. Joanne Bradley, who sat behind me raised her hand and offered that perhaps the third secret would reveal when the world would end. Our class had some knowledge on this subject after having read the apocalyptic prophecies of John in the Book of Revelations, the final book of the New Testament.

Sister Elizabeth Mary called on a few other classmates. I raised my hand, smiled at Fred, and winked. Fred looked at me wide-eyed, his eyebrows arching high. He silently mouthed, *"Don't do it, Walt!"*

Sister Elizabeth called on me. I stood to speak. "Actually, Sister, the third secret was the check for the Last Supper. After the apostles had their share of bread and wine, they bolted on poor Jesus and left him holding the tab. And Jesus, well, since he was Jesus, did not carry money and this left him in a very tight spot."

The air in the classroom was devoid of sound. Fred stared at the ceiling and then crossed himself. Joanne Bradley let out a tiny giggle and that was enough to trigger an explosion of laughter from the rest of the class.

I knew I was in trouble before I saw the expression on Sister Mary's face. She glared at me with a look of disbelief. Her eyes bulged. The pallor of her face changed from a pallid gray, to crimson, to a purplish red. I thought her face might burst out of the starched white tunic that covered her neck and boxed in her head.

She rushed down the aisle toward me, grabbed me by my hair, pulled me out of my desk, and pushed me to the rear door of the classroom and then across the hall to her office where she shoved me into a chair. She opened her top desk drawer and pulled out a twelve-inch round paddle that had several small holes drilled through it.

On the wall behind her desk were several framed pictures of martyred saints: John the Baptist's severed head on a platter being presented to Roman ruler Herod Antipas, St. Sebastian tied to a post with his chest riddled with arrows, and St. Daniel sitting in a den surrounded by several hungry lions.

Sister Mary waved the paddle back and forth like a batter on the sidelines in a baseball game. I figured she was warming up her arm.

"Why are there holes in the paddle, Sister?"

She shot me a wicked smile. "To defy gravity, Mr. Madigan. Please, hold out your hands, palms up."

I held out my right hand, palm up, and Sister Mary brought her paddle down with lightning speed. *Whack! Whack! Whack! Whack! Whack!* It happened so fast, I didn't register the pain right off. In short order, it burned as though she had placed a hot iron on my palm.

"Left hand, please," Sister Mary said. "Palm up."

Whack! Whack! Whack! Whack! Whack!

Tears of pain streamed down my cheeks. I managed to smile at Sister Mary and asked, "Are we done here, Sister?"

"Yes, we are done for now, Mr. Madigan. But the next time you disrespect the name of Jesus, it will be ten whacks on each palm!"

Sister Mary directed me to return to the classroom while she stayed in her office. I prayed she wasn't calling my mother. When I returned to my desk, the classroom was very quiet with the exception of a few muffled laughs disguised as throat clearing.

After being batted, my hands swelled to the size of baseball mitts. I couldn't even pick up a pencil. Fred looked at me and his expression said it all: *I tried to warn you, Walt.* He had, of course, and I should not have made the comment about Jesus being stiffed by the apostles. Maybe, just maybe, next time I would think twice before blurting out comments for the amusement of my fellow classmates. Then again, knowing myself, that probably wouldn't happen.

Chapter Twenty-Five

Burn Ward

Temperatures began to drop as the sun descended on its westward trek. A cool breeze blew in from Tokyo Bay, and a light chop danced across the water. I thought about Lt. Coleman and the last time I assisted him at the 106th Hospital. We had finished our rounds at 0200 on the third floor. Lt. Coleman mentioned he had been assigned extra duty that night to cover for another CQ medical officer who was out sick.

"Not sure if you want to assist me on this one, Madigan," he said.

"No problem, L-T. I'm a night owl anyway. I enjoy assisting you on your rounds."

He looked at me wearily. "Have you ever been to the second floor of this hospital where they transport the burn victims?"

I had heard rumors about the horrors of the burn ward. The Army transported the burn patients to the 106th, mostly in the middle of the night when the temperatures were cooler and hospital activity was minimal. I took a moment to let his words sink in.

"If you can handle it, Lieutenant, then I think I can."

Lt. Coleman loaded up his medical cart with supplies. We walked down one flight of stairs and had to carry the cart as there were no elevators. Upon entering the burn ward, the first thing that hit me was the smell. *Oh, Jesus,* I thought.

When I worked at the Pico Center Market as a box boy in my early teens, one of my chores was to flatten cardboard boxes and put them in the dumpster out back. Butchers from the meat department also used the dumpster to discard meat scraps, and if the day was hot, the stench of rotting meat was almost unbearable and sure to make me gag. Smell is a potent reminder. I steeled myself as I experienced the same sensation as we entered the ward. Overhead lights were dimmed and I was glad the bay was equipped with good air-conditioning.

The burn ward was populated by members of all military services and held about seventy beds. Injuries were sustained from explosions, accidents, and that dreaded gelling agent, napalm. There were Army infantry grunts like me, some from the First Cavalry Division, some from the Big Red One, and a few sailors who suffered burns in an accident on a destroyer in the Tonkin Gulf off North Vietnam.

In large part, this bay held badly burned Marines who were overrun by the enemy in a Central Highlands battle. The Commanding Officer called in napalm and the F-4s got a little too close to the friendlies.

I was surprised to see that the ward was a hive of activity at that hour with staff comprised of doctors, nurses, corpsmen, and volunteers like myself. Limp, dirty, and soiled bandages that had been applied on the battlefield were carefully removed, and afterward, the patient was immersed in a big tank, a bath that started the daily cleaning and debridement, that is, the removal of damaged skin.

I cringed inside at the groans coming from these men who experienced great pain. There was plenty of morphine being administered; however, I could tell it wasn't having much effect on those with the most severe burns.

Corpsmen worked in tandem, wrapping fresh gauze around arms, legs, and heads. They saturated the gauze with liquid silver nitrate, a known antiseptic that caused a chill and subsequent shivering that lasted ten minutes or so. Some of the men had no hands, no arms or legs. For lack of a better description, the ward resembled the set of a Hollywood mummy film from the 1930s.

Lt. Coleman went from bed to bed to regulate the IV drips so that the men would stay hydrated, a key factor in burn recovery. The L-T could do the task without assistance, and rather than watch, he encouraged me to talk to some of the patients to try and boost their morale.

Looking around, I saw some of the corpsmen were joking around with the burn patients as they applied fresh bandages. *If they can do it, I can do it,* I thought. My eyes scanned the room of patients.

Before I set off, the L-T took me aside. "Remember, no war stories. Why don't you tell these guys about your dance with Jill St. John? That will cheer them up. And, most importantly, give them hope."

I walked up to a bed where a soldier was covered head to toe in white gauze. There were two open black holes for his eyes, two black holes for his nostrils, and his mouth was a larger black hole in his white bandaged head. I glanced at his chart on the side of the bed and saw his name and rank, Marine Corps Lance Corporal Alan Summers. Thankfully, his hands were not burned so I reached for his left hand and introduced myself.

"Lance Corporal Summers, I'm Private First Class Walter Madigan. I'm assisting Lt. Coleman tonight. He doesn't need my help right now so I thought I would visit with you and tell you a few stories about my growing up in Southern California."

The Marine made a short, throaty sound.

"I know you have trouble talking and you don't have to say anything. I'll do all the talking. Here's an idea—I'll tell you what. Can you squeeze my hand?" He responded with a squeeze. "Okay, good. Give my hand one squeeze to stop if it's too much, and two squeezes for yes, keep going. Should I continue buddy?" I felt two squeezes.

"All right, then. I'm going to tell you about my senior prom in high school and my fifteen-second dance with actress Jill St. John." I launched into the story.

Two weeks before graduating from St. John Vianney, I attended my senior prom. I double-dated with my best friend, Bob Edwards. My gracious sister-in-law, Frances, let us borrow her new maroon 1965 Chevrolet Corvair for transportation. She also picked up two corsages for our dates.

My brother, Kelly, pulled me aside and slipped two twenty dollar bills into my hand. "For your late night dinner in Malibu after the prom," he said. Bob and I had rented tuxedos. We felt very dressed up and adult for this special occasion.

Bob Hope's son, Kelly, was in our senior class, and Mr. Hope decided our prom should be at the fabled Beverly Hills Hotel on Sunset Boulevard where he would act as emcee. The Beverly Hills Hotel was famous for playing host to Hollywood royalty over the years. It was Tinsel Town's playground since Beverly Hills was born. The hotel opened in 1912. It was beautifully landscaped, surrounded by twelve acres of tropical gardens and exotic flowers. It was dubbed the Pink Palace by the local celebrities who often vacationed there.

As we exited Sunset Boulevard and entered the long driveway up to the hotel, Bob said, "Remember to tip the valet, Walt."

I had no idea what a valet was, and joked, "Isn't a valet one of those guys who wears tights and prances about on the stage in those satin square-toed shoes?" Our dates giggled.

(Two squeezes.)

"That's a ballet, you idiot," Bob said." They don't have self-park in a joint like this, and please, Walt, don't ask the valet if he has change for a dollar." We heard more giggles from the girls.

Valet parkers at the Beverly Hills Hotel were men in their late teens and early twenties. They were decked out in white pants, white tennis shoes and a pink golf shirt with the hotel name embroidered across the left breast pocket. Every attendant was handsome, lean and fit, and looked as though he could have been an extra in Central Casting. We approached via a circular driveway that led to the hotel entrance, and I slipped the valet three dollars as we exited the vehicle.

The entryway to the hotel was clad in plush red carpet as if we entering a theater for the Oscars. Overhead, the *porte cochère* was painted in green and white accents. The lobby was oval-shaped and decorated with exotic plants and plush sofas. Soft lighting from a multi-colored crystal chandelier that was shaped like a giant inverted ice cream cone glowed from above. There was no expense spared. Oddly, what really caught my eye was the banana leaf wallpaper plastered throughout the hotel.

"Exotic indeed!" my date, Patty, commented. "So this is how the other half lives, right, Walt?"

(Two squeezes.)

As we entered the hall leading to the Grand Ballroom, we saw a sign positioned on an easel stating the prom would begin at 7:00 p.m. We were half an hour early, and Bob suggested we check out the legendary Polo Lounge north of the lobby.

The Polo Lounge was originally a children's restaurant when the hotel opened. It was refashioned as a bar/restaurant in the early 1940s and got its name from a celebrity band of polo players who played in the bean fields nearby.

Entering the restaurant, I noticed the subtle array of colors: peachy pinks, apricot, and yellow accents. The walls were decorated in green fern wallpaper and were backlit at the base of the booths with hidden soft lighting. The ceiling was candy-striped in white and green. We chose a table for four near the bar.

"Drinks anybody?" Bob asked.

"Yeah, right, Bob," I said. "We may be dressed in tuxedos and our dates look lovely in their gowns, but we still look eighteen. I doubt we will be served alcohol."

Bob shot me a look of hyperbolic disdain. "Oh, ye of such little faith, my boy. Let me handle the drink orders. Ladies, how about pink champagne?" Patty and Michele smiled and nodded their heads in agreement. "Walt, name your poison."

"Okay, Bob, bourbon and Coke."

Bob assumed an air of supreme confidence when approaching a delicate situation, for example, ordering drinks in the Polo Lounge when we were underage. He was also a major bullshitter, but a convincing one.

Bob sauntered up to the bar and approached the middle-aged bartender who wore dark slacks, a starched white shirt and a green tie, a green vest that matched the green fern wallpaper, and a name tag that read: Mickey.

"What's your pleasure, sir?"

"Hi, Mickey," Bob said as if they were old friends. "I'm Bob Edwards. Pleased to meet you." Bob reached across the bar to shake Mickey's hand and complimented him on his spiffy outfit.

"We are here tonight as chaperones for the senior class prom hosted by Bob Hope. His son, Kelly, is in the senior class. We are from the class of '62 and the Principal of St. John Vianney, Father Vincent Cavalli, asked if we would be so kind as to volunteer our services as chaperones. Then he winked at Mickey and continued, "You know, in case any of those Catholic boys get out of line."

Oh, my God, I thought, as I listened to their conversation. *Bob is up to his knees in bullshit.*

(Two squeezes.)

"Pink champagne for our dates, a bourbon and Coke for my colleague, Walt. And I'll have a Seven and Seven."

"Yes, sir," Mickey said. "I'll have them ready and bring them to your table in a moment."

Bob returned to our table and gave me a look with all the insouciant charm he could muster. "You know, Walt," he said. "Sometimes life is all about taking chances."

We entered the Grand Ballroom at 7:30 p.m. after enjoying several drinks in the Polo Lounge. Classy decorations were festooned throughout the room in our school colors: maroon, gold, and royal blue. Above us, a large revolving ball covered with small gold mirrored facets projected swirling patterns of light across the walls and dance floor.

Bob Hope stood front and center on the stage with his trademark golf club straddled across his right shoulder. He was in the process of doing his usual comedy shtick when we noticed his outfit: a traditional black tuxedo jacket, starched white shirt, black bow tie, and to the delight of the crowd, blue and white seersucker shorts, and men's garters holding up his black socks. Kelly, his son, wore the same outfit and it generated several laughs. Bob Hope provided the band for our entertainment. They played cover songs of popular groups such as the Beatles, the Beach Boys and the Righteous Brothers.

Midway through the prom, Bob Hope took to the stage and announced he had a big surprise for us. "Ladies and Gentlemen, please welcome, Jill St. John!"

Every senior gasped when Miss St. John walked on stage and gave Mr. Hope a little peck on the cheek. She looked every bit the glamorous movie star, dressed in a pink chiffon strapless gown with beaded rhinestones above the waist. The dress was form-fitting and accentuated her tiny waist and ample breasts. Her face was perfectly symmetrical with high cheekbones, a straight nose, and a defined jawline. Her gown's color complimented her coiffed red hair and hazel eyes.

She held the microphone and greeted the senior class with a dazzling smile; I had never seen teeth so white and perfect.

Bob Hope said a few words about Jill St. John's career and plugged an upcoming film she was starring in.

"And now, Ladies and Gentlemen," Mr. Hope continued. "I have another surprise for you. Please welcome, recording star, Jack Jones!" Thunderous applause followed. Jack Jones came on stage, shook Bob Hope's hand and kissed Jill St. John on the lips. It was rumored they were engaged.

Jack Jones took the mic and greeted the senior class. Then he belted out several of his hits: "Lollipops and Roses," "Wives and Lovers," and "Call Me Irresponsible." Rather than follow current rock and roll trends, Jones was a pop singer, and stayed true to the big band/swing variety. When it came time to crown the King and Queen of the prom, he crooned "The Impossible Dream." The King and Queen danced alone for several seconds before other couples joined them on the dance floor.

As we danced, I noticed Miss St. John stepped down from the stage and approached couples, tapping the senior on the shoulder, and politely asking if she could cut in. I'm sure Bob Hope put her up to it because next, she tapped his son, Kelly. She danced for all of ten or fifteen seconds and then moved to the next couple while Jack crooned on. Then my blood pressure shot up and my heart started beating like a tiger on the run; she was heading my way!

"She's getting close, Walt," Bob mused. "Better break out your breath spray, pal."

I was slow dancing with my date. I closed my eyes and started my negotiations with God Almighty. *Dear God, please let her tap my shoulder*

*and in return,…one hundred Our Fathers,…no, five hundred Our Fathers,
five hundred Hail Marys, three hundred Glory Bes, ten novenas,…*

Then something wonderful happened—Miss St. John tapped my
shoulder.

"Mind if I cut in?" she asked Patty.

Up close, she was even more drop-dead gorgeous. Her makeup
was applied to perfection, her amazing hazel eyes, photogenic face,
and pouty Cupid's bow mouth, sent me to the moon. In other words,
she was a goddess, exuding beauty from every pore.

She didn't need to ask twice as I left Patty aside—okay, I gave her
a little push—and I placed my right hand around Jill St. John's waist
and held her right hand with my left.

She laughed. "You're feeling frisky tonight…," she looked at my
name tag, "Walt."

"It's not every night I have the pleasure of dancing with a woman
as beautiful and glamorous as you, Miss St. John."

"Call me Jill. By the way, you look very handsome in your blue
tuxedo jacket."

I pulled her in a little tighter and was surprised she didn't resist. I
caught a whiff of her perfume and felt my knees grow weak. I felt she
was coming on to me, so I blurted out, "Miss St. John, uh, Jill, if you
were any more beautiful, I might go into convulsions and collapse
right here on the dance floor. You would probably have to put a stick
in my mouth so I wouldn't swallow my tongue."

Jill backed away and let go of my left hand. She looked startled, as
if she thought I was getting ready to ask her to marry me. "Nice dancing with you, Walt," she said as she hurried on to the next couple.

"So there you have it, Corporal Summers, my fifteen seconds of bliss
with Jill St. John. I thought for sure she would have a change of heart

and find me later. I could imagine her putting a note in my hand: Meet me at midnight in the Polo Lounge—alone. But, alas," I sighed. "That didn't happen. And my date, Patty, wasn't happy about being pushed aside when Jill asked for the dance. Oh, well."

(Two squeezes.)

Lt. Coleman was finishing his rounds and nodded at me to wrap it up. I squeezed Lance Corporal Summers's hand, and said, "I'm going back with the L-T soon, but before I go, remember, you will be returning soon to The World, Corporal. You're going back to a place where people love you, and they will care for you in the coming months and years, and make sure that you heal properly. You have fought bravely for your country, and you should be proud of your accomplishments. You will never see the face of war again in your lifetime. Without a doubt, you are the bravest Marine I have ever met. In fact, you were brave enough to listen to my prom night story," I quipped.

(Two strong squeezes.)

"Stay strong, Marine, and may God be with you on your journey home."

Chapter Twenty-Six

Father Bill

"Everything okay there, soldier?"

The familiar voice jolted me out of my reverie. I looked up from my bench and saw a man smiling at me. He wore a tan officer's uniform with tiny gold crosses on his lapels.

"Ah, Father Bill. You startled me; and yes, everything is fine."

"Mind if I join you for a few minutes, Private Madigan?"

"Sure, Father, have a seat."

I moved aside on my bench to make room for the chaplain. He held his Bible and I assumed he was on his way to the 106th Hospital for his nightly rounds. He sat down and passed me a handkerchief that I used to wipe the tears streaming down my face.

"I heard the good news, Private. You're leaving tonight for the states, right?"

"Yes, Father, 2100 hours from Tachikawa. Tomorrow I will wake up at Travis Air Force Base in California. But today is the best day of my life. I thought I was going to be reassigned to my unit in Vietnam. I even scrounged a pair of fatigues and boots from the supply sergeant. No way was I going back to Charlie Company wearing these dreaded blue pj's." I laughed. "Looks as though I will be wearing them a bit longer. The orders said further evaluation at Travis of shrapnel wounds in left hip/buttock area and lower legs. The orders were signed by the Chief Medical Officer of the 106th, and I also noticed Lt. Coleman's signature. You have no idea of the joy flowing through me right now."

"Oh, I can imagine, Madigan. It's like you are getting a second chance at life. Remember what I said to you a few weeks ago about God testing each and every one of us. Well, you have been tested by God in a most profound way, not only on the battlefield, but on the wards of the 106th. Lt. Coleman said you were a great help assisting him on his rounds, and that you told stories and gave words of hope to the wounded soldiers. He also told me about the night in the burn ward. Sometimes, Private, God rewards us when we least expect it."

"'Press down and everflowing,' as my mother used to say."

"Come again?"

"'Press down and everflowing.' It's a phrase from the New Testament, either Matthew or Luke. I don't remember. And knowing my mother she probably mangled the wording. Basically, she told us kids that the verse is all about helping a person who is less fortunate than you, and displaying generosity and kindness, and when you do that, God will eventually reward you."

Father Bill let this sink in, and we sat in silence. The sun had set and the sky had turned salmon pink near the horizon deepening into dark blue above. A star low on the horizon twinkled like a beacon, a guiding light for the path back to The World.

"Of course." Father Bill nodded and the corners of his lips turned up.

"What's that, Father?"

"Your mother may have mixed up the wording, but she got the meaning right. The verse comes from Luke 6:38." He opened his Bible and read the quote to me. " 'Give and gifts will be given to you; a good measure, packed together, shaken down, and overflowing, will be poured into your lap. For the measure with which you measure will in return be measured out to you.' Your mother sounds like a good woman, soldier. She did a good job raising you."

"Thanks, Father. She is indeed an amazing woman. She raised me and seven other siblings, and made sure we had a good Catholic education. I can't wait to see the expression on her face when I walk through the door of our little house on Marvin Avenue."

Once again we sat in silence watching the last colors of the sunset unfold over Tokyo Bay. The water reflected the sky and shone a palette of gold and red tints. A flotilla of magenta-tinged clouds paraded across the horizon and a few more stars appeared.

"There's so much beauty in this world, Father. I just don't understand why we go to war."

Father Bill considered what I said and sighed. "I wish I had an easy answer for you, soldier, but I don't. Man has been warring against himself for millennia. The old debate of nature versus nurture rages on. When psychology emerged as a science in the early part of this century, it focused on nurture, the environmental cause of behavior."

He talked a while about the ideas presented by the behavioral psychologists who sprang up to herald the nurture side of the movement whereby learning from outside forces provided the basis for a person's development. He brought up environmental factors of why man goes to war, such as geography, politics, and economics.

"Then you have those who believe in the inherent forces of man's nature," he said. "Do certain men harbor evil intentions in their biological makeup? Is it in their DNA? It seems that way to me.

"Are you familiar with the book *Silent Spring* by Rachel Carson?"

"I've heard of it."

"Well, she wrote that man is a part of nature, and therefore, his war against nature is inevitably a war against himself. Even the apostle

Peter wrote: 'I urge you, as strangers and aliens in the world, to abstain from the sinful desires that war against your soul,' (Peter 2:12)."

"Thank you, Father," I said. "That's a lot of information to absorb. When I get back to The World and eventually leave the Army, I plan on going back to college. I'd like to study the concepts you discussed, maybe I'll even major in psychology. I need to discover these answers on my own."

It was time for me to return to Building C barracks to get ready for my trip home. We stood up. Father Bill shook my hand and then gave me a hug.

"Good luck with the next phase of your life," Father Bill said. "I know it may be hard at first, but try to look back at your experiences in war with a positive light. Think about it this way: you adapted to extremely stressful situations and because of it, you became resourceful. Try and extrapolate that wisdom to all phases of your life in the years ahead and, well, you'll do fine."

"Thank you, Father."

When I got back to the barracks, I saw the tan packet with the reassignment orders on my bunk. I decided not to open it; I already knew what was in there. Instead, I grabbed my shave bag and went through its contents. Every possession I owned could fit in that shave bag: a few razors, shaving cream, toothbrush, and other assorted toiletries, my dog tags, a wallet I purchased at the commissary with my new military ID, a tattered paperback copy of *Goldfinger* by Ian Fleming, my Purple Heart, and the rosary my mother gave me when I departed for Vietnam. It occurred to me that all of these items were replaceable, but the one thing that wasn't replaceable was the greatest gift that God had bestowed on me—my life.

I was the only soul in the barracks. The other soldiers were either at the mess hall or the NCO club. I turned off the overhead light and walked up to the window behind my bunk. Looking eastward toward the Pacific, I could make out the silhouette of the Boso Peninsula in the dwindling light. The ocean was black and the evening sky had dissolved into deep hues of indigo. It was a clear night and above the horizon the heavens were peppered with a billion stars. A crescent moon rose in the northeast.

In a matter of hours I would be on the C-141 Starlifter, flying out under those twinkling stars, and like Corporal Summers, heading back to a place where people loved me, to family and friends who would welcome me home.

I returned to my bunk, lay down in the darkness, and waited for the medics to come and take me away.

Acknowledgments

I owe a debt of gratitude to the Post Traumatic Stress Disorder specialists at the VA Hospital in Reno, Nevada. One man in particular, John Keely, a PTSD psychologist, became a confidant and special friend. John conducted a writing class on the side, a sort of Rorschach test, if you will, to determine what lies beneath the rough exterior of veterans with severe PTSD. Fortunately, my case was mild. I had been writing in my journals for years and shared them with John. He loved my writing and encouraged me to transpose the journals into chapters and to eventually create a memoir. The rest, as they say, is history.

I give a special mention to my editor, Janet F. Williams of Good Day Media, who worked tirelessly on my chapters even when she was struck with the dreaded Covid-19. A meticulous editor, Janet fixed every sentence, polished each word like a precious gem, put them back together in a sensible order, and created a narrative that flowed evenly and shined like the sun—no easy feat since the story continuously jumps back and forth in time.

I would be remiss if I didn't mention my fellow boonie rats in Charlie Company, 2nd Battalion, 7th Infantry, First Cavalry Division (Airmobile). Men such as Jeff Porter, Leland Roach, Randy Kent, Randy Caswell and others, who always had my back since my first day as the FNG (fucking new guy) in Charlie Company. We managed to keep hope flowing through our veins, sharing stories of our youth, sometimes whispering to each other in the inky blackness while out on night ambush patrol. I would not have made it back to The World without their undaunted courage and grace under pressure.

And finally, to The Father, Son and Holy Spirit.

About the Author

Walt Madigan was born in Los Angeles, California in May 1947, the sixth of eight children brought into the world by Nellie Madigan. He attended Catholic schools through grade 12 and was drafted into the United States Army in 1966. He served as a combat infantryman in Vietnam, was wounded twice, and finished his second year in the Army as a Drill Sergeant at Fort Ord in Monterey, CA. He received an Honorable Discharge in August 1968.

After earning a degree in Behavioral Sciences from San Jose State University (1972) and moving to Alaska where he learned the flooring trade, he opened his own business, North Shore Flooring, first in North Lake Tahoe, and then in Kings Beach, CA. He specialized in antique, vintage and reclaimed hardwoods, fine carpeting and luxury vinyl plank until his retirement in 2019. He lives in Arroyo Grande on the Central California Coast. His days are now filled with writing exercises, pickleball, kayaking on the ocean, and day hikes in Big Sur.